GEORGE S. PATTON

GEORGE S. PATTON

A Biography

David A. Smith

GREENWOOD BIOGRAPHIES

GREENWOOD PRESS
WESTPORT, CONNECTICUT · LONDON

YA
B
PottG

Library of Congress Cataloging-in-Publication Data

Smith, David A.
   George S. Patton : a biography / David A. Smith.
      p. cm.—(Greenwood biographies, ISSN 1540–4900)
   Includes bibliographical references (p.) and index.
   ISBN 0–313–32353–4 (alk. paper)
   1. Patton, George S. (George Smith), 1885–1945. 2. Generals—United States—
Biography. 3. United States. Army—Biography. 4. United States—History, Military—
20th century. 5. World War, 1939–1945—Campaigns. I. Title. II. Series.
E745.P3 S65   2003
355′.0092—dc 21
[B]   2003048520

British Library Cataloguing in Publication Data is available.

Library of Congress Catalog Card Number: 2003048520
ISBN: 0–313–32353–4
ISSN: 1540–4900

First published in 2003

Greenwood Press, 88 Post Road West, Westport, CT 06881
An imprint of Greenwood Publishing Group, Inc.
www.greenwood.com

Printed in the United States of America

The paper used in this book complies with the
Permanent Paper Standard issued by the National
Information Standards Organization (Z39.48–1984).

10 9 8 7 6 5 4 3 2 1

Always dear to your heart,
Strife, yes, and battles, the bloody grind of war.
What if you are a great soldier? That's just a gift of god.

The Iliad, *1:209–211*

CONTENTS

Photo essay follows page 54

SERIES FOREWORD

In response to high school and public library needs, Greenwood developed this distinguished series of full-length biographies specifically for student use. Prepared by field experts and professionals, these engaging biographies are tailored for high school students who need challenging yet accessible biographies. Ideal for secondary school assignments, the length, format and subject areas are designed to meet educators' requirements and students' interests.

Greenwood offers an extensive selection of biographies spanning all curriculum related subject areas including social studies, the sciences, literature and the arts, history and politics, as well as popular culture, covering public figures and famous personalities from all time periods and backgrounds, both historic and contemporary, who have made an impact on American and/or world culture. Greenwood biographies were chosen based on comprehensive feedback from librarians and educators. Consideration was given to both curriculum relevance and inherent interest. The result is an intriguing mix of the well known and the unexpected, the saints and the sinners from long-ago history and contemporary pop culture. Readers will find a wide array of subject choices from fascinating crime figures like Al Capone to inspiring pioneers like Margaret Mead, from the greatest minds of our time like Stephen Hawking to the most amazing success stories of our day like J. K. Rowling.

While the emphasis is on fact, not glorification, the books are meant to be fun to read. Each volume provides in-depth information about the subject's life from birth through childhood, the teen years, and adulthood. A thorough account relates family background and education, traces per-

sonal and professional influences, and explores struggles, accomplishments, and contributions. A timeline highlights the most significant life
events against a historical perspective. Bibliographies supplement the ref-
erence value of each volume.

PREFACE

I would dare to say that most people have heard the name George S. Patton. Those who know military history are familiar with him and his actions, of course, but Patton is renowned among ordinary Americans in a way that few of our generals are. After Robert E. Lee and "Stonewall" Jackson (both of whom were heroes to Patton), after George Washington and Patton's contemporary Dwight Eisenhower, one inevitably comes across George Patton in the hallowed halls of American military leaders. Some would say that Patton should be rated as high as number four on the all-time list. Like Lee and Jackson and Washington, Patton continues to captivate.

As is the case with so much in modern American culture, Hollywood has made a fictionalized version of George Patton far more familiar to us than is the actual man. Once you see the movie *Patton*, and George C. Scott's singularly captivating portrayal of the general, it becomes difficult not to see Patton striding around on that stage, in front of a huge American flag, giving his famous speech to the troops. Except that it's George C. Scott we envision, not George S. Patton. All this is not necessarily a bad thing, though. It has kept his image, personality, and accomplishments in the public consciousness far better than otherwise may have been the case. *Patton* won seven Academy Awards in 1970 including Best Picture, Best Actor, and Best Director, taking its place among the all-time greats. Because of this, the movie, and by an odd kind of cultural osmosis, its subject, remain part of the American cultural lexicon. But the movie, however, despite its attempts to show the many different sides and contradictions of Patton, is limited by time in what it can tell us, and still tends, therefore, to oversimplify the man.

Existing along with all the familiarity, there is something uncomfortable to many Americans about Patton. Despite an overall coarsening of the culture, a squeamishness remains about a man who faced his job so matter-of-factly. Perhaps it is even becoming more pronounced. But war meant—and always will continue to mean—killing and Patton had no desire to sanitize that central fact. War had to mean killing, and killing in vast numbers. The army that killed more of its enemy faster and more efficiently usually won the fight. A tough fact, but there it is. Americans like their military heroes, but the dirty business of killing sometimes gets lost in the discussion of honor, valor, sacrifice, duty, patriotism, and the like. We can talk about those concepts and see them on copious display in our heroic generals, and can then go on about our lives drawing inspiration from these admirable qualities without ever even drifting into the more unpleasant business of killing enemy soldiers that war inevitably entails. We seem to like our generals more if they are removed a couple of steps from the actual bloodletting of combat. Dwight Eisenhower was a hero of World War II and one of the most popular presidents of the twentieth century. The vision of Ike that sticks with most people is his famous grin. That's a long way removed from combat in Europe, but then again, Ike was a planning general. He never led troops into combat. There's that sanitized military leader that we can embrace.

The Robert E. Lee familiar to most Americans, on the other hand, is an older man with a graying beard, sometimes sitting on his horse Traveler, sometimes standing on a front porch. What pulls us to images of Lee are his eyes. They look kind and sad and tired. They were. He was. The gentleness of his face helps us remove him from the dreadful carnage of the battlefields which those kind eyes surveyed for four long years. But Lee picked those fields and directed that his men fight and die on them by the tens of thousands. Just like that, his kind image begins to waver. Lee's nemesis Ulysses S. Grant, on the other hand, who gained a reputation for spending the lives of his troops so liberally, makes us a little more uncomfortable from the start.

George Patton is far more difficult for us not just because he saw lots of combat but because of the apparent fact that he loved it so. He did love it. There was no place that he would rather have been than in the heat of battle. When he explains to fresh young men new to the war that their job is to "kill devastatingly" and "effectively," and that "battle is the most magnificent competition in which a human being can indulge," our sensibilities tend to bristle. What are we to make of this? How is this admirable? It's a tough puzzle.

No matter what the cynics say, most Americans like to think of themselves as a peaceful people. It was a tough job to take young men from the middle America of the 1930s and 1940s and teach them to be killing machines. Patton knew the job was tough, and that's why he spent so much time giving his profanity-laded pep talks to new soldiers. Their job was going to be harder than any of them realized and it was his job to make them soldiers and to explain to them that the world of the soldier was radically different than the world of the civilian. The best way to return to being a civilian, however, short of a devastating injury that sent you home for the course of the war, was to get the war over as quickly as possible. And the way to do that was to kill devastatingly and effectively. Patton believed that the way to end the war was to win it. The quicker his soldiers defeated their enemies, the quicker the war would be over, and the quicker they could go back to being civilians again. There is a simplicity about it that we sometimes tend to overlook. We do so, however, at the cost of making people like Patton seem monstrous to us. There are unpleasant tasks to be carried out and we have special people called soldiers to do them. They do what they do and we can appreciate their sacrifice, but one of the lesser realized services they provide is keeping we, the people, removed from the nasty business of fighting and killing to preserve freedom and win wars. To study Patton is to see this business up close. That our sensitivities are heightened by the luxury of peace and comfort makes it more difficult for us. But that's our problem, not his.

War is, and rightly should be, a last resort. It was for Patton, too, but he recognized that sometimes war was inevitable, and when it was, there was little use in fretting over it. Talking about peace was fine, often it was even admirable, but Patton coldly believed that war would always be with us. As such a constant companion to humanity, going back at least as far as the Bible and the ancient Greeks, and, we can assume, back even further, it is a condition to be managed. Patton the avid historian knew this to be true. Through all of his knowledge of history and warriors of the past, Patton believed that there was only one way to fight a war: fight it hard and fight to win. It would be horrible while it went on, but like he told his soldiers, the harder one fought, the sooner it could be over. The way back to middle America was through Berlin.

A note on some of Patton's writing is in order. At the beginning of each chapter there is a little excerpt from one of Patton's many poems he wrote over the course of his life, or an excerpt from a prayer that he composed. These give little glimpses into Patton's mind that we don't really get in any other place. He would say in poetry, for instance, things he would never say in conversation. As any historian, I have also used his actual

words to describe his actions and thoughts whenever possible. That pres-
ents a distinctive challenge when you're working with Patton. He was a
notoriously terrible speller. Some biographers attribute it to dyslexia,
some figure that he was just poorly educated and never took the time to
learn to spell. No matter what the cause, I have replicated his spelling precisely the way he put it down in his letters and diary entries. While it is,
admittedly, often annoying to the modern reader, it is likewise an ever-
present reminder of his particular intellectual difficulty. He certainly
knew he had this problem, and as he got older, was even able to poke fun
at himself. "Any idiot can spell a word the same way time after time. But
it calls for imagination and is much more distinguished to be able to spell
it several different ways as I do." Earlier in life, however, such an attitude
was harder to maintain. His troubles created a blend of persistent self-
doubt but a burning desire to force himself to succeed. Since Patton's
spelling is so consistently adventurous I am leaving off the constant edi-
torial [sic] after each misspelled word to avoid further hindrance to the
reader.

The vast majority of all the quotations of Patton in these pages comes
from the two volumes of *The Patton Papers*, vol. I and II, edited by Martin
Blumenson. Copyright © 1974 by Martin Blumenson. Reprinted by permission of Houghton Mifflin Company. All rights reserved. These two
volumes are an exhaustive collection of Patton's letters, writings, lectures,
articles, and diary entries. The other major source in which the information in these pages—including most of Patton's poetry—is found in *Patton: A Genius for War*, by Carlo D'Este. Copyright © 1995 by Carlo
D'Este. Reprinted by permission of HarperCollins Publishers Inc. All rights
reserved. This is a magnificent biography. These works are all but indispensable in understanding George Patton. I comment further on them,
and on some other works, in a short bibliographic essay at the end.

Also in order is a word or two about military terminology, especially
that which applies to battle formations and groups. The smallest unit with
which we will regularly deal here is the regiment. Simply put, regiments
together form brigades; brigades together form divisions; divisions then
make up a corps; several corps together form an army; and armies working
together form an army group. For example, a total of 42 divisions organized into six corps served under Patton's Third Army from August 1944
to May 1945. The number of soldiers in each unit can vary tremendously,
but in 1943, the average infantry division was made up of about 14,200
soldiers. An armored division had slightly fewer men, about 11,000.

As does any author, I have accumulated many people to whom I owe a
great deal of thanks over the course of writing this. First of all, my grati-

tude goes to Kevin Ohe and Lynn Wilson at Greenwood Press. Kevin initially got in touch with me about this project and patiently waited for it to
arrive on his desk. Lynn helped see it through to completion. My friends
and colleagues in the History & Political Science department at High
Point University in High Point, North Carolina, especially Rick Schneid
and Rick McCaslin, were very helpful in getting me started on the road to
writing about Patton and military history in general. Their writing sets
very high standards in this field that I will always strive to follow. Lieutenant Colonel Larry Burnett of the Army ROTC post at North Carolina
A&T University in Greensboro helped me understand the organization
and responsibilities of armored cavalry regiments and armored divisions,
and the way these units work together. The people in the history department and in the administration at Baylor University have been very welcoming and supportive in my first year here, and have taken a genuine
interest in my work. As always, my family has been the primary source of
strength and support that allows me to follow through on projects like
this. My parents, Leo and Barbara Smith, have always been behind me in
all my endeavors and have taught me what loving and encouraging parents are. My wife Lorynn has loved and encouraged me and kept me going
through years of happy marriage and cross-country moves. She's listened
to me talk about Patton more than anyone should ever have to. I don't
know how this would've been completed without her, and for this and for
many other things I'm very thankful to her.

David A. Smith
Baylor University
Waco, Texas

TIMELINE

11 November 1885	Born in San Gabriel, California.
August 1902	Meets sixteen-year-old Beatrice Ayer for the first time at Catalina Island, California.
September 1903	Enters the Virginia Military Institute in Lexington, Virginia.
June 1904	Transfers to the U.S. Military Academy at West Point, New York.
June 1905	Repeats his first year of studies due to poor grades.
June 1909	Graduates from West Point and is commissioned a Second Lieutenant in the Cavalry.
September 1909	Reports for his first duty assignment at Fort Sheridan, near Chicago, Illinois.
26 May 1910	Marries Beatrice Ayer.
December 1911	Transferred to Fort Myer, Virginia, just across the Potomac River from Washington, D.C.
May 1912	Selected to represent the United States in the Modern Pentathlon in the 1912 Olympic Games to be held in Stockholm, Sweden.
July 1912	Participates in the Olympics. Places fifth in the overall Pentathlon.
July–August 1912	Following the Olympics, studies fencing and swordmanship in France. He returns for more study in the summer of 1913.
September 1913–June 1915	Attends and graduates from the Army's Mounted Service School at Fort Riley, Kansas.

September 1915   Assigned to duty at Fort Bliss, Texas, near El Paso.

March 1916   Enters Mexico with the U.S. Army's Punitive Expedition, chasing Pancho Villa. Serves under General John J. Pershing.

May 1916   Leads a wild shoot-out with some of Villa's subordinates. Promoted to First Lieutenant later in the month.

February 1917   Punitive Expedition returns to United States from Mexico.

April 1917   U.S. enters World War I.

May 1917   Appointed Commanding Officer, Headquarters Staff, American Expeditionary Force.

28 May 1917   Sails for Europe.

November 1917   Assigned to the new and experimental Tank Service.

December 1917   Opens and heads up a U.S. tank school at Langres, France.

September 1918   His tank corps participate in the St. Mihiel offensive. Later that same month, the corps takes part in the Meuse-Argonne offensive.

26 September 1918 Is seriously wounded in the Meuse-Argonne offensive and spends several weeks in hospitals. (Eventually he is awarded the Distinguished Service Medal, the Purple Heart, and the French "croix de guerre" for his actions.)

11 November 1918   World War I ends on Patton's thirty-third birthday.

March 1919   Returns to the United States with his men.

1923–1924   Attends the Army's Command and General Staff College, Fort Leavenworth, Kansas. Graduates with honors.

1925–1928   Assigned to staff duty in Hawaii.

1931–1932   Attends Army War College, graduates with distinction.

1932   Returns to duty at Fort Myer, Virginia as the Executive Officer, Third Cavalry Regiment.

1938   Spends time as Executive Officer of the Academic Division, Cavalry School, Fort Riley, Kansas. Promoted to Colonel. Ends year as Commanding Officer of the Third Cavalry Regiment, once again back at Fort Myer.

1 September 1939 Germany invades Poland; World War II begins.

July 1940   Appointed Commanding Officer, Second Armored Brigade of Second Armored Division, Fort Benning, Georgia.

1941   Promoted to Major General and appointed Commanding General, Second Armored Division.

7 December 1941   Japan attacks U.S. base at Pearl Harbor; U.S. enters World War II.

January 1942   Appointed Commanding General, First Armored Corps.

Spring 1942   Establishes the Desert Training Center for tank and mechanized infantry combat training in the deserts of Southern California.

August 1942   Sails for London, England, to participate in planning for U.S. invasion of North Africa.

8 November 1942   U.S. forces invade North Africa in Operation TORCH. Patton commands Western Task Force landings in Morocco.

March 1943   After American defeat at Kasserine Pass in Tunisia in February by the German Afrika Korps, Patton is put in command of the U.S. Second Corps in hopes of revitalizing it and avoiding further battlefield losses. By the end of the month, U.S. forces have gained a victory in the battle of El Guettar.

April 1943   Returns to Morocco for continued planning of the upcoming invasion of Sicily.

10 July 1943   Invasion of Sicily, code named Operation HUSKY, begins. Patton commands U.S. Seventh Army in the invasion.

August 1943   While visiting troops in hospital, Patton slaps soldiers he thinks are shirking their duty with imagined injuries. Outcry against Patton erupts. Removed from all meaningful battlefield commands until further notice.

January 1944   Transferred to England.

March 1944   Appointed Commanding General, U.S. Third Army, for Allied campaign in Northern France. (Until Third Army becomes operational, though, Patton makes himself seen around southeastern England as part of a ruse to misdirect German anticipation about upcoming invasion location.)

6 June 1944	American, British, and Canadian troops storm the beaches at Normandy, France.
6 July 1944	Arrives in France.
1 August 1944	U.S. Third Army becomes operational in France.
16 December 1944	German counter-offensive Battle of the Bulge begins.
11 January 1945	Units of Patton's army break through to surrounded American troops at the small village of Bastogne.
28 January 1945	The Bulge in the allied lines is finally eliminated.
March 1945	Crosses the Rhine River into Germany with his men.
9 May 1945	World War II in Europe ends.
9 December 1945	Is seriously injured in an automobile accident.
21 December 1945	Dies in a hospital in Heidelberg, Germany.

Chapter 1

ANCESTORS AND EXPECTATIONS

The roar of the battle languished
The hate from the guns grew still,
While the moon rose up from a smoke cloud
And looked at the dead on the hill.

The battle had begun early in the morning near the banks of a little creek just east of town and had raged on until around 5:00 in the afternoon, when at last the badly outnumbered defenders finally began withdrawing. They pulled back through the town and headed south, leaving thousands of casualties strewn across the fields and roads and in the mud of the creek. The smell of gunpowder and smoke still hung in the air as the sun began to disappear behind the mountains just west of town. Now everything was quiet. Medics and soldiers from the victorious army walked the field, checking for any survivors among the wounded. Among the 2,000 captured prisoners was a colonel who had been badly hurt as an exploding artillery shell tore up his hip. His captors carried him into town where a doctor looked him over and pronounced the wound serious, but probably not mortal. Despite the best precautions, however, a bad infection and a high fever set in. Six days later, George S. Patton was dead.

This particular George S. Patton was a colonel in the Twenty-second Virginia regiment, the battle came to be called the Third Battle of Winchester, and the year was 1864. Colonel Patton had come from a prominent Virginia family and was relatively well known in the state, but it would be the dead colonel's grandson who would become one of the most famous soldiers in all of American history. While the grandfather had led a regiment up and down the Shenandoah Valley of Virginia, the grandson would lead an army across France and into Germany. The grandfather served under the famous Thomas "Stonewall" Jackson, the grandson under the even more famous Dwight D. Eisenhower. It was the experience of the grandfather, though, with a valor and bravery magnified down through the years that became a model of the ideal soldier that would always weigh heavily on the grandson, a man who would also be named George Smith Patton.

Like many American families, the Patton family of Virginia was able to trace its ancestors far back into history. Further, in fact, than the history of the nation itself. The first Patton to come to America came to the Virginia colony from Scotland as an indentured servant around 1769. Robert Patton worked for the multimillion-dollar tobacco exporting firm of William Cunninghame and Company that had paid for his passage across the Atlantic. Once in Virginia, Patton quickly gained a reputation as dependable and a hard worker. Before his term of servitude had expired, he was put in charge of the company's operations in the little crossroads town of Culpepper.

When the term of his contract was up, he was free to travel and go wherever he wanted. He moved thirty miles southeast to Fredericksburg, which had emerged as an important port town on the Rappahannock River and the center of the area's agricultural business. George Washington's family had owned a farm nearby and his mother Mary Washington still lived in town when Patton arrived. He settled down as an independent merchant and eventually became a leading importer of things like salt, wine, rum, molasses, coffee, sugar, and pepper. When the American Revolution broke out shortly after he arrived, he did not join up to fight in the Continental Army; but afterwards was still regarded as an upstanding citizen who, at times, served on the town council, was a trustee of the local charity school, and even was the man the town depended on to organize the annual Fourth of July celebration.

Just as his lack of service in the war did not prevent him from having a high reputation in the community, neither did it keep him from marrying the young daughter of a war hero. Hugh Mercer, like Patton, an immigrant from Scotland, was a prominent physician who lived in Fredericksburg and who most likely would have known Robert Patton. Mercer also knew George Washington well, the two friends having fought against the French on the frontier together back in 1755. More recently, Dr. Mercer had tried with sadly limited success to treat his old friend's epileptic stepdaughter. In the early years of the Revolution, Mercer became one of George Washington's most trusted Generals. In January 1777, when his little daughter Anne was not yet three years old, Hugh Mercer was killed by the British at the battle of Princeton. His loss touched Washington and his hometown deeply. Years later, in October 1792, Anne Mercer married forty-two-year-old Robert Patton.

Within just a few years, the Pattons had started a large family. Apparently space in the Patton household was quickly at a premium, for at some time around 1800, Robert had a new house built—one that reflected both his growing family and his high social standing in Fredericksburg. Sitting on five acres at the northern edge of town, White Plains, as the house became known, had fifteen rooms, three chimneys, and high marble columns on the front porch. It was right on the road coming into town and an indication of Patton's success as a merchant and standing in the town. Now, at last, they had enough space for the family.

In all, the Pattons would have seven children, including an infant son who died before his first birthday. Their third son was named John Mercer Patton and was born in 1797, shortly before the move to White Plains. Though Robert was always content to spend the rest of his years as a leading merchant in Fredericksburg, his son John grew up to study law and served nine years as a Virginia congressman. Eventually he moved to Richmond, became a leading attorney in town, and was elected to the Executive Council of Virginia four consecutive times. He was once even acting governor for thirteen days in 1841 after Governor Thomas Gilmer resigned. John M. Patton was a very well-known citizen and most who knew him were fond of him, even though he had a tendency to dominate any conversation. A generally good-natured man, he loved to eat and he loved to talk.

John Patton had an even larger family than his father and mother. He and his wife Peggy had twelve children—three daughters and nine sons. They also owned some land they called "Spring Farm" northeast of Richmond near Culpepper, where his father had worked as an indentured servant decades before. Like many other prosperous families with land, the Patton's had some slaves. As far as their descendents were concerned, however, probably one of the most important decisions they ever made had to do with their sons' education. Four of the nine attended the Virginia Military Institute (VMI) in Lexington. Their first son to graduate from VMI, John Mercer Patton, Jr., did so in 1846, just seven years after the school opened its doors.

John and Peggy Patton's fourth son, born in 1833, was named George Smith Patton and was the second of the boys to go off to VMI for school. His younger brother Waller Tazewell followed three years later. William, the youngest of the Patton boys, was the last to head off to Lexington. All three studied under and got to know the eccentric professor of physics,

Thomas J. Jackson, and the school's first superintendent, Colonel Francis Smith. When George graduated in 1852, he stood second in his class and was thinking of being a teacher when he moved back to Richmond. Like his father, however, he studied law and eventually decided to make it his career also. Just over three years after graduation he married and ten months later George S. Patton and his wife Susan had their first son whom they named George William. A daughter Ellen came along the very next year.

George Patton and family soon moved to Kanawha County in what is today West Virginia and he began practicing law in Charleston. Much like his outgoing father, George became a highly regarded member of the community in addition to being quite a successful lawyer. He was known about town for his dashing and chivalrous behavior toward the ladies and for the sharp way he always dressed. In all, he was "the charm of the social circle, where his genial wit, sparkling humor, ready repartee, and ringing laugh made him ever welcome." He was also a very religious man who could be found in church every Sunday morning.

His world was not strictly limited to Charleston, however, and throughout the 1850s he saw all too clearly that his country was drifting closer and closer to a war between the states with each passing year. Neither did George Patton lose the notion of service and military responsibility that VMI had installed in him. Shortly after he came to town, he put together a volunteer militia company made up of upstanding young men just like himself. He even put his obvious fashion sense to work, designing the company's bright uniforms for which they, in part, became known. What else set them apart was their precise drilling. Patton put his men through marching practice, close-order drill and weapons handling, just as he himself had experienced at VMI. Known throughout the area as the Kanawha Riflemen, they took part in parades and various social affairs, where, as one of the members described it, they would find themselves standing guard over the fried chicken and lemonade.

But not all was pomp and ceremony. In October 1859, when antislavery fanatic John Brown and 18 followers raided the federal arsenal at Harper's Ferry in hopes of inciting a slave rebellion, the Kanawha Riflemen were one of the first Virginia militia groups to respond. Patton and his men traveled by train over 250 miles from Charleston across part of the Appalachian Mountains to the picturesque little town where the Shenandoah and Potomac Rivers met. Arriving on the scene from the opposite direction was army Colonel Robert E. Lee, in temporary command of a detachment of almost 90 marines sent to restore order. It was George Patton's first opportunity to see Lee in action.

In April 1861, after fighting between the North and the South broke out at Fort Sumter, South Carolina, Patton called an emergency meeting of the Kanawha Riflemen. In the group's official statement in response to Abraham Lincoln's call for 75,000 militiamen to put down the rebellion, the men from Kanawha County vowed they would never take up arms against Virginia. On the contrary, they were ready and willing to answer the call to defend their state, and were soon integrated with other units like theirs into a complete Virginia regiment, the Twenty-second. Down in Richmond, Waller Tazewell Patton was a member of the secession convention and George took his son to see his uncle Waller take part in the historic vote that decided Virginia should leave the union. That night, there was a torchlight parade through town in celebration. In a referendum held on May 23, the voters of Virginia supported the convention's decision to secede by a four-to-one margin.

As war fever spread, many in the extended Patton family relocated to Spring Farm where John Patton's widow Peggy still lived. George Patton and all of his brothers, except the alcoholic eldest, marched off to war. Over the course of the next few years, brothers Hugh and James were wounded at Second Manassas and Cold Harbor, respectively. Brother Isaac was among those captured when Vicksburg surrendered in the sweltering July of 1863. That same month, Waller Tazewell died from wounds he received while taking part in the renowned Pickett's Charge against union positions on Cemetery Ridge on the third day of the Battle of Gettysburg.

For his part, George fought mainly in Western Virginia, serving part of the time under Professor Jackson—now known everywhere as "Stonewall"—and within thirteen months had been wounded twice. Once, when informed that his broken arm would need to be amputated, he drew his pistol and threatened to shoot anyone who tried to do so. As soon as was humanly possible after he had been wounded, he was always back out in the field with his regiment. Meanwhile, his family, including young George William, moved from place to place, and often Susan Patton would serve as a nurse. Once when they lived across the street from a field hospital, the boy saw cart loads of arms and legs being hauled off in the wake of countless emergency amputations. For the rest of his life he would remember following his mother around as she tended to wounded men and recall her fainting from the horrible smell of the dead.

By late 1864, George and the Twenty-second Virginia were part of General Jubal Early's Confederate Army of the Valley, defending the Shenandoah Valley. To keep Early's army away from Washington, D.C., Ulysses S. Grant sent a formidable force under General Philip Sheridan to drive Early back up the Valley and to cause as much damage as he possibly could while doing so. That September, the two armies met at the third major battle that was fought near the little town of Winchester, Virginia. At some point in the hard fighting out toward the left flank, Colonel Patton rallied his men to defend against a cavalry charge. Shells burst all around him, and ultimately his position was overrun. As the sounds of battle faded and Early's troops retreated up the Valley, one of Sheridan's officers came across the gravely wounded Patton and arranged for him to be taken into town for care.

Although she had no way of knowing it, Susan Patton had been a widow for four days when she first learned of her husband's fate from a Union newspaper. By the time she reached Winchester, he had been buried. His horse, saddle, and sword stayed in the family only because his personal servant Peter avoided capture by the Union patrols strewn across Virginia and stealthily traveled with them back to Patton's older brother John, Jr.'s house. The devastated Susan spent the rest of the year near Richmond, worrying also about their newborn daughter, not yet a year old.

In the wake of the war, Virginia was a devastated land. Fields were laid waste; once grand homes were in ruin. Susan gathered her children and their possessions and moved out toward Orange, Virginia, where she and at least three other members of the extended family moved into an old mansion once owned by James Madison's brother. Even though they had a roof over their heads, their outlook was bleak as they tried hard to farm the land. Susan worried constantly about how she would look out for her children and guarantee them a future brighter than the present.

The answer soon arrived in the form of a letter and would completely uproot the Pattons from Virginia. A year and a half after the war ended, Susan heard from her brother Andrew Glassell, a lawyer living in southern California. He sent Susan $600.00 and encouraged her to bring her family west and join him. It seemed to be the best hope the family had, and she jumped at the opportunity even though the money fell well short of what was necessary for the move. She began selling off family possessions, only refusing to part with her late husband's sword, saddle, watch, and Bible. In November 1866, she and her family boarded a steam ship and began the long journey to a fresh start in California.

As Susan's oldest child, ten-year-old George W. Patton worked hard to help his mother support the family. Even though he grew to love sunny California and became fast friends with Uncle Andrew's seven children, he missed Virginia and longed to return. He also, naturally, missed his father. Within a couple of years, he decided he wanted to change his name to honor the man whose sword and saddle remained treasured keepsakes, and in 1868 George William Patton became George Smith Patton II.

There were other changes in the family, too. That same year a familiar face arrived in Southern California from Virginia. It was the late Colonel Patton's old friend and VMI classmate George H. Smith who, like so many others, had left the South in the years after the war came to an end. He spent time in Mexico and San Francisco before settling in Los Angeles where he began to practice law with Andrew Glassell. It was not long before he and Susan were spending more and more time together and in 1870 they were married. Their family grew to six as they had two children together in addition to Susan's four. George H. Smith helped raise Susan's children as if they were his own. In the evenings, he would captivate the younger George with stories about the bravery and heroism in battle of the father he had never really known.

Young George was a good student who worked hard on his studies and regularly made the honor roll. Still, he missed Virginia—or at least he missed the Virginia of his stepfather's stories and his own dim memories. He longed to return and eventually got a chance. Each year the Virginia government made it a policy to appoint to VMI sons of the school's graduates who had been killed in the war, and in 1874 George entered the school.

After graduation, he lingered in Lexington for a year teaching tactics and French, but soon he was back in California, studying law with his stepfather and his uncle. He became a well-known young man in and around Los Angeles, which had become something of a boomtown by this time. As a young, handsome, single man in a prosperous law firm, he moved in influential circles, and occasionally drifted toward politics, serving for two years as district attorney.

Before long he had set his sights on a young woman from one of southern California's leading families. In December 1884, he married Ruth Wilson, daughter of Benjamin Davis Wilson. "Don Benito," as he was known, was a man famous throughout the region, whose adventurous life had taken him from Tennessee to the wild southwest, when it was still part of Mexico, and from there to southern California. Along the way he fought against the Mojave Indians, served against Mexico in the Mexican War, ran a huge cattle ranch, was instrumental in starting the southern California citrus industry, served as mayor of Los Angeles, planted the first vineyards in the surrounding valleys, built the first Episcopal church in southern California, and served in the state senate twice. His land holdings ran to over fourteen thousand acres and the winery he operated, along with his vineyards, was at one point the largest in the entire world.

Benjamin Wilson had died in 1878. In subsequent years after he joined the family, George Patton gradually took over running much of the Wilson family's property and businesses. The newlyweds lived in a large ranch-style house known as Lake Vineyard. It wasn't long before the first family addition came along. On November 11, 1885, their first child was born. He was a boy, and they named him George Smith Patton, Jr.

Chapter 2

BOYHOOD

First there's the boy
Unapt by nature he for aught of hardship
Yet his early mind perverted by untruthful literature
He sees a picture of war glorified
And longs to be a soldier.

Sadly, like so many infants in the nineteenth century, little George Patton, Jr. was sickly and weak through his first months. The family nurse, in fact, feared for his life, but the worries eventually passed and the child grew into a strong and healthy boy. George S. Patton, Jr. was born into a comfortable family and through his early life, rarely knew want or even unhappiness, if his own recollections are to be believed. Within a few years a second child was born—a girl they named Anne.

Shortly after George was born the family moved to a house in Los Angeles so his father would not have quite as far to travel to go to work. Still, most of George's early memories came from the rambling Lake Vineyard house. The family still spent much of its time there, and the ranch house was always teeming with action, for many relatives still lived there full-time. George's grandmother Margaret Wilson lived there, along with his unmarried aunts Annie Wilson (who became known in the family as "Aunt Nannie") and Susan Patton.

For a young boy, Lake Vineyard must have been something close to a wonderland of adventure. The dusty attic was full of swords, saddles, guns, canes, books, and who knew what else. There were lots of horses around, too. George had one named Galahad and one named Marmion and he learned to ride them using his grandfather's saddle. He loved to brush and groom them, and sometimes at night he would slip out to the stables with his dog Polvo and just lay in the hay, thinking he must be the happiest boy in the world.

Along with learning to ride, young George also learned to shoot, and he took particular pride in his marksmanship, especially when his father would take him goat hunting out on Catalina Island. By the time he was 12 he was accomplished with both rifles and shotguns. He trapped squirrels, fished, camped out, and learned to sail.

On quieter evenings, his father or Aunt Nannie would pull a book from the shelves and read from the classics like the *Odyssey* or the *Iliad*, stories of Alexander the Great, Plutarch's *Lives,* or Xenophon's *Persian Expedition.* George especially liked to hear stories of Napoleon. As it was for many who grew up in the nineteenth century and before, John Bunyan's *Pilgrim's Progress* was very influential with its tales of good and evil and the dangers of temptation. Above all, the Bible was the central text in Patton's early life, and Aunt Nannie, especially, read it to him unceasingly. He absorbed its lessons and morals and developed an unshakeable faith in God and love of the Bible that would remain prominent elements of his character for his entire life. Aunt Nannie also instilled in him the habit of getting down on his knees to pray.

All his heroes, however, were not from the Classics or the Bible. Far from it. In fact, few role models were more pervasive in the Patton household than Confederate Generals Stonewall Jackson and Robert E. Lee. From time to time his stepgrandfather would come by the house and young George would marvel at the tales he heard about the illustrious heroes of Virginia and, often even more stirring, the grandfather he never knew. Another regular guest in the Patton home was the infamous Confederate cavalry leader John Singleton Mosby, who now lived in California and worked as an attorney for the Southern Pacific Railroad Company. Between Grandpa Smith's tales of Colonel Patton's bravery in combat, reverent tales of Jackson's bold marches and Lee's unequaled leadership, and Mosby's recollections of his legendary raids, little George was steeped in stories of valor in battle and the adventurous life of the soldier. The honor and tradition of the Virginia Military Institute and its graduates, many of course closely related to George, also figured prominently in all the stories and taught him how important these virtues were in forming a man's character.

Life was full of horses and dogs, adventures both real and imagined, and the unswerving love and support of his mother, father, and aunt. His parents and Aunt Nannie tended to be overly lenient with little George and he was rarely punished severely, even when one of his pranks or make-believe adventures resulted in property damage.

The whole family spent much of its recreation time on Catalina Island, just off the coast of Los Angeles. Father and son would hunt, fish, swim, and sail in both summer and winter. Many of the region's wealthiest families built extravagant vacation houses on the island, while other visitors stayed at hotels. Being for the most part between these extremes, the Patton's owned a small cottage on Catalina.

Despite his early exposure to books and his father and aunt reading to him almost constantly, it became evident to his parents early on that young George was having serious trouble learning to read. Writing and spelling, too, seemed to be nearly insurmountable challenges. While no one could have labeled it so at the time, it is quite possible that the young boy suffered from dyslexia. Throughout his life, he would remain aware that he was deficient in these areas, often referring to himself as stupid and lamenting his inability to learn. It was not until he was 11, when many children of his age were already in the fifth grade, that he started to read and write and his father enrolled him in a school. This late start to his formal education and the lenient attitude of his parents toward his early learning might well have contributed to his lifelong problems with spelling almost as much as any learning disability he may have had. "The Classical School for Boys" was in nearby Pasadena and was operated by Dr. Stephen Clark. The two dozen or so students were, like George, from prominent Southern California families and spent their time learning mathematics and geometry, reading and composition, history and geography, and French, German, Greek, and Latin.

Despite his difficulties, George labored hard at his studies. Proper spelling remained a constant problem, but aside from that, his writing became clear and precise through almost non-stop practice. While mathematics gave him trouble, he especially excelled at history, in which he liked to study the motives, behavior, and the character of numerous military leaders from the ancient world. To young George, studying such things was simply an extension of his own fascination with the subject and was fed by countless days at playing soldier and countless nights listening to the tales of his own ancestors' valor, bravery, and sacrifice. Small wonder he took to it so.

Even at this early stage, George's school compositions reveal much about him, his attitudes, and his beliefs. He was developing a distinct drive to succeed and he seemed to admire and identify with those from history who most clearly exhibited such a similar drive. "Alexander the

Great was one of the most ambitious men who ever lived," he wrote when he was fifteen. "From his early youth he always tried to excell. . . ." When he thought about Alexander's dashing cavalry charge it was easy for him to remember the exciting tales told by veterans like John Moseby and all the stories about his brave and daring grandfather on whose saddle he had learned to ride. "No man ever so truly wanted the title of great as did Alexandor," he wrote on still another occasion. "From his earliest years he always aspired to perfection in everything." George could have easily been writing about himself.

Young George also illustrated a surprisingly good understanding of military tactics, principles of maneuver, and ideas about how to handle an army. He wrote of Greek battle lines shifting into position for the battle of Marathon, tactics between warring Scottish clans, and knights of the Middle Ages storming castles. The Greek general Epaminondas emerged as one of his favorites. He was "with out a doubt the best and one of the greatest greeks who ever lived, with out ambition, with great genius, great goodness, and great patriotism; he was for the age in which he lived almost a perfect man." In every famous leader, however, he thought that he could sense what he called "the undefinable difference which makes a good or a great general." The behaviors and actions that brought about this undeniable difference became second nature to him.

The teenage years of every young boy or girl are filled with turning points, even though relatively few of them are able to grasp the import of some of these important moments as they happen. For George Patton, 1902 was a year of great importance. In August, he met his future wife, and it was love—or at least a resounding crush—at first sight. Her name was Beatrice Ayer, and her wealthy, prominent Boston family, which was distantly related to the Patton's via a marriage, was out in California from Massachusetts vacationing on Catalina Island. Beatrice, George, and six other cousins as they called themselves entertained the combined families and their guests by putting on a play. As the Ayer's returned east in the fall, Beatrice was thinking of George as the family paused in Colorado. "I wonder if Georgie shot any very large goats at the island," she wrote in a letter to her Aunt Nannie. She added that she hoped he would not get homesick if he were to go away to school. That Christmas, she sent him a tiepin and they exchanged letters in January. Even though they would have no more contact for over a year, neither forgot the other.

The year 1902 was also momentous because by the end of the summer George had decided he wanted his life's work to be that of a soldier. He could imagine no better career. He did not, however, plan to enlist—that was no option for the son of such a wealthy and socially visible family. Instead, and by no means surprisingly, he wanted to become an officer. By far and away the best entry for this route then, was to attend the U.S. Military Academy at West Point in New York. Upon graduation, he would be commissioned as a second lieutenant in the army. Getting into West Point, though, was the tricky part. Each cadet had to be appointed by a senator, a congressman, or the president, and although the number of annual appointments had been increased in 1900, only 150 cadets were still admitted each year. Even after securing such a prized appointment, a cadet still had to undergo a rigorous physical and mental exam, plus demonstrate mastery of a host of academic subjects. Going to West Point was a tough proposition, even before one arrived at the gates.

In September, then, Patton's father began writing letters to begin the process. Over the next year and a half, he would write dozens of letters to various officials hoping to secure one of the coveted appointments. Most of his efforts were concentrated on Senator Thomas R. Bard from California, who, Patton discovered, would be able to appoint a new cadet some time in 1904. Patton was not alone, however, in supporting his son's attempt. Several prominent figures that were friends of the Patton family took part in the campaign as well. For months Bard was deluged by letters supporting the character and military fitness of young George S. Patton, Jr. At least 14 different bankers, judges, physicians, attorneys, leading California businessmen, and even an aide to the governor wrote to vouch for the young man. All described his character and mental fitness in the most glowing terms imaginable. Many pointed out his proud military lineage, a consideration Senator Bard claimed to take very seriously indeed. "A young man who has reason to be proud of the military services of his ancestors may be depended upon for trying to maintain the honorable reputation of this family," he replied to one of the many letters implying this very point.

Still, the process was competitive, and Patton's father was worried whether his son had had enough formal education to measure up against other candidates. When Bard made it clear that some sort of examination would be necessary to make his final decision, Patton despaired. And even if his son did get the appointment, he would still have to pass yet another examination, this time at West Point itself. Should he send his son to a special preparatory school, he wrote to the superintendent. Not necessary, came the reply. "Any young man who has availed himself of the school opportunities afforded throughout our country need not fear the entrance examination for West Point," explained the head of the academy, "as it accords with the subjects covered in the public schools of the country at the minimum age of admission." Maybe this would have been comforting to anyone else, but not to young George's father. The boy's education was limited at best—only six years now, and that at a private institution—and Patton did not kid himself about his son's shortcomings.

Perhaps there should be some sort of alternate plan if a military academy appointment fell through. He decided on an obvious second choice: VMI. Generations of Patton men, including himself, had graduated from the Virginia Military Institute, and while it did not provide the automatic commission as an army officer upon graduation, chances were good that a VMI graduate could get one. Getting young Patton admitted to VMI was a foregone conclusion and his father arranged for him to begin there in the fall of 1903. Then, if the appointment to West Point could be secured for 1904, a year at VMI would do away with having to undergo the Academy's own admission exam.

In September 1903, the family took the train east to Virginia. Once at VMI, Patton excelled. He judged it a good omen that the measurements for his uniform exactly matched those of his father and grandfather. Even though he sometimes complained about the rigors and lamented the lowly status that freshmen—rats as they were called—held at VMI, he presented himself immaculately groomed and dressed, and made high academic marks. He joined the Kappa Alpha fraternity and focused as hard as he could on being a good soldier and a good student. Even though his father had hoped he'd put it off for a year, Patton joined one of the second-string football teams and played left tackle. He knew he wasn't very good, but he played as hard as he could, and the experience did give him "the fighting spirit of that great institution."

Despite George's successes at VMI, neither he nor his father ever stopped thinking about West Point. In almost every letter home he urged his dad to keep up the pressure on Senator Bard. "Bother him until he gives it to me," he wrote. His father had no intention of letting up and eventually his hard work on behalf of his son began to pay off. In February 1904, Patton learned that he was to return to California so he could take Senator Bard's competitive examination. He spent six days on a train headed west across the country and he studied as hard as he could the whole way out. On February 15, he took the exam. For the entire six days on the train back eastbound, he worried nonstop about how he had done.

That the results came back quickly was a great relief to both father and son. The news was wonderful. On March 3, Mr. Patton received a short telegram from Bard saying that he had nominated George Patton to be a new cadet at West Point. As soon as possible Mr. Patton needed to let the war department know where it could reach young George. Patton immediately wired back his gratitude and sent word to his son. The *Los Angeles Times* announced the news the next day.

At VMI, George Patton was thrilled at the news. He was grateful for all his father had done, and "as for Bard I rank him and the pope on an equal plane of hollyness." A classmate helped him write a formal letter of thanks to the senator. In less than two months he went to Fort McHenry in Baltimore for a physical exam and late in May, he received a letter from the war department ordering him to report to the United States Military Academy at West Point on June 16, between 8:00 A.M. and noon.

Chapter 3

BECOMING A WARRIOR

And now we sing not of the stage of life
But of that stage of which there is no counterpart on earth
The stages of the life of a cadet.

Patton's father came east to accompany his excited son up to New York. On the way, they stopped at Richmond and walked some of the Civil War battlefields east of the city. From time to time, the journey must have seemed like a pleasant vacation and Patton must have spent time imagining the armies of blue and gray struggling over the hills and slogging through creek beds, smoke from musket fire and artillery hanging in the air. Just as surely, did the task at hand always crowd back into his mind as he wondered what might await him once he arrived up north.

Incoming freshmen at the U.S. Military Academy at West Point must report in June for what amounts to a lengthy and arduous orientation process. Known informally now as "Beast Barracks" the process was called "Plebe Camp" back in 1904. Cadets were in for weeks of hard work, hard marching, and no small amount of general harassment by third-year classmen who oversaw much of the plebes' activities. Patton hadn't been there a month before he was overheard to remark that the way he had stood at attention at VMI was a lot tougher than how they did it at West Point. Here they seemed to be easier on things like keeping eyes to the front and whispering in the ranks. The upperclassmen who heard of his remarks quickly convinced him of his mistake. By August he had been written up for seven demerits. Still, he initially believed that he was being treated better than he had been down at VMI. The food was good and he was especially appreciative that they had dessert two times a day.

The work was hard, though, and there was little letup for the cadets. Reveille blew at 5:30 every morning and there was nonstop action until taps at 10:00. Free time was limited to Sundays unless one wanted to rise extra early. By mid-July the plebes were out of the barracks and in tents, drilling and marching and going out on maneuvers. He drilled with artillery and machine guns, but most often just with infantry alone. If a cadet somehow found himself with a free moment, he was expected to use the time to clean his rifle. At night, Patton wrote letters by the light of a single candle when he wasn't pulling guard duty. He grew to regard the five-by-eight-foot tents as actually more comfortable than the barracks, even when it rained, especially because there were no bedbugs in the tents and he had netting to keep out mosquitoes.

As the summer wore on, he began to dread the prospect of classes starting and worried about whether his academic performance would be good enough. He had been commended at times for his actions on maneuvers and in general felt more comfortable with his abilities in the field than in the classroom.

One night when he was walking guard duty for the camp, three older cadets whose responsibility it was to catch a plebe dozing on duty came rushing at him from out of the darkness. They tried to get his rifle away from him, but Patton threatened to bayonet the first one who came within six paces. Unknown to Patton, they had secretly released the catch on his bayonet earlier in the evening. This was a good thing, too, because in all likelihood, had they not done so, he might well have killed one of them during the short melee that ensued. As it was, Patton rammed the barrel of his rifle into one's stomach so hard it sent him sprawling on the ground. The three quickly slipped away to test the rest of the plebes on guard duty. When they came back by later, "they halted at the proper distance and did not fool with me." He thought that word of his tough action against the upperclassmen must have gotten around quickly, "for when later in the evening a ghost came round he visited every post but mine." Whether he was correct or not in thinking that some of the upperclassmen had begun to respect him, if not to like him, he made it through the first half of August with only two demerits. He began to stand out from the others because of his soldierly bearing.

As was the tradition, a big crowd gathered to see the plebes march back to the barracks from their time in the field. As he passed in front of the commandant's quarters, he enjoyed the feeling of all the eyes on him. More and more he was sensing that he was at an important place. "The absolute honor of this place is amazing," he wrote to his father. "There is nothing but truth here."

The honor that he felt in being a cadet affected him in a couple of ways. First, it magnified the sense of duty, honor, and pride that his parents had instilled in him from his earliest years. From time to time the pride he felt triggered a snobbishness to surface in him. It also tended to make him easily annoyed by people who either did not behave the way he believed they should or who did not seem to take the duty and honor that came with being a West Point cadet seriously enough. Secondly, his surroundings sent him into periodic bouts of self-doubt and deep insecurities over his abilities and whether or not he was ever going to make something out of his life.

Before he had been at West Point two months, he had witnessed two funerals for generals who were buried in the academy's cemetery. The somber pageantry embodied all his ideas and preconceptions of military honors and tradition. The muffled drums, the Long Gray Line marching in its raincoats, the volleys of salute cracking in unison from a line of rifles, all captivated him. He was convinced it was worth going into the army if only to get a military funeral. His love of military history and this feeling of institutional honor and pride mixed so thoroughly that he could easily see himself in scenes throughout time and project himself into events that had more in common with ancient history than with his contemporary surroundings. "I would like to get killed in a great victory," he said after watching the latest funereal spectacle. His image of having "my body born between the ranks of my defeated enemy escorted by my own regiment" seemed more in line with ancient Roman or medieval warfare than with the clash of armies in the dawning twentieth century. No matter. Patton's notions of duty, honor, and chivalry would always make him feel much more at home in his historical imagination than in his modern surroundings. That he learned to fence and handle a sword in his freshman year—and quickly grow to love it—fit his image of himself perfectly.

Related to this in a way were his occasional ugly bouts of snobbery. In some of his remarks, one can hear the attitudes both of his wealthy California family and his historic Virginia roots. Early on, he complained that there were not as many gentlemen like himself in evidence in his plebe class. His first two roommates were not refined enough for his tastes, but "unless I can find some other fellows who are gentlemen and also students, I may room with these two all year." In fact, the only young men he found who met his definition of gentlemen were Southerners. He thought it best to room with them for "if I were to room with some common man even if he were a student I could not go about with him and I would not like to live with one class and go about with another," he explained to his father.

His sense of being set apart, of belonging to a different class, was wrapped up in his ideas of duty and, as odd as it might sound to modern ears, a burning ambition not as much to get ahead as to give himself over completely to doing his duty successfully. His passionate, consuming idea of duty was related to the chivalrous image he had of his ancestors, and these ideas of chivalry further fed his already pronounced tendency, namely, elitism. Elitism and duty wrapped up so tightly together that they were inextricable in his mind. He had a duty because of his elite heritage and he was elite because he bore this chivalrous sense of duty. The feeling made him aloof and extremely disdainful toward most people who did not, for whatever reason, live up to his ideas of responsibility and duty. All his life, he would have trouble controlling his bitter scorn for the man who did not do his duty. It could cloud his judgment, overcome his good sense, and cause him to lash out in frustration. It could jeopardize his entire career.

Strangely existing alongside of this, however, was a nagging sense that he would never be good enough to succeed in his mission. He complained that he did not concentrate well and sometimes feared that he was nothing more than a "darned dreamer with a willing spirit but a weak flesh," the type who always intends to be a success but never quite achieves it. He guessed that there was no one in his entire class "who so hates to be last or who tries so hard to be first and who so utterly fails." Such intolerance for his own failures—and those of others—would be a strong element in his character all his life.

When he had trouble with his grades, it magnified these feelings. English gave him the most difficulty. As he would later in life, he sometimes blamed those around him for his failures. His English teacher "was a scoundrel and did not like me so he consequently gave me low marks," he rationalized. After Christmas he began studying French, which also was hard for him. His spelling remained poor. He usually did much better in math, although taking tests was often a dreaded ordeal in which he sometimes fell short. He did well in tactics because he liked it and studied harder for it.

By April, however, Patton was dropping little hints in his letters home that he might have to repeat his first year. Like any other student who goes through such circumstances, he began to have a hunch early on, and sense the inevitability before it became official. Time and time again since September he had said he didn't think he would be turned back as it was called, but now in the spring it seemed more and more likely. He tried to put a brave face on the matter, saying perhaps it would be better in the long run if he was turned back, but the disappointment was crushing. He dreaded telling his father even though he knew his father and mother would be as supportive as ever. In June he sent a simple telegram to his father breaking the news. It must have been a difficult telegram to write. He was coming home. There was a slight reprieve, though. He was not being turned out of the academy entirely. The academic board instead recommended that he return in the fall to join a new fourth class.

Through all the stresses of his first year, his parents stood by him resolutely. In countless letters his father encouraged him, sympathized with him, maintained that everything would come out fine in the end, and let his son know that no matter what, he and his mother loved him and supported him unquestioningly and faithfully. Such support kept Patton going. He would always have a great need for this kind of vocal praise and endorsement, and tended to lapse into depression when it wasn't forthcoming from his superiors.

In Patton's first year at West Point, there were some triumphs along with the defeats. He found that he excelled in the study of tactics and that he was one of the best in his class at swordsmanship. In terms of soldierly behavior, he was regarded as outstanding. He played on the football team—although not on the first string—and ran track. In March 1904, the cadets traveled to Washington, D.C., and marched in Theodore Roosevelt's inaugural parade and attended an inaugural ball. He had a wonderful time.

Patton's mother and father were not his only source of encouragement and affection. In the midst of everything else, Patton had kept up a long-distance courtship of Beatrice Ayer. She sent him little gifts like a silver soldier watch fob, although with his typical insecurity he hoped "there was no hidden sarcasm in it and that she did not mean I was a tin soldier." He sent flowers for her coming out celebration in December. Because she and her family lived in Boston, Beatrice was able to come to Washington for Roosevelt's inaugural celebrations, and to dance with Patton at the ball. She, too, was supportive when the bad academic news broke, and encouraged Patton to keep at it. Even though their relationship was carried on primarily through letters, Patton fell head over heels in love with her. He thought that she was "the best thing in her line in the world," and "I swallowed her hook to a swivle (as one says of a fish)," he confessed to his father. At the start of the next academic year, he officially asked her to be his date at every dance given at West Point "from now until I graduate."

In August 1905, shortly before he headed back to the Academy, Patton began to keep a journal. It wasn't really a diary but in it he jotted down phrases and ideas that reflected his beliefs, military principles, and guidelines, and he even began to write poetry. He turned twenty during his second year at West Point, and his grades were markedly improved but he found that repeating still another year as a plebe (his third, counting his year at VMI) was "hard on a patrician like me and getting pretty wearisome." Obviously he still thought of himself from a higher class than many of his fellow cadets although it did not keep him from getting more involved in extracurricular activities. He made the third team playing football, but in short order had suffered a grievous injury and was laid up in the academy hospital. A description in the yearbook summed it up well: "Two broken arms bear witness to his zeal, as well as his misfortune, on the football field." He was released from the hospital, however, in time to attend the annual Army-Navy football game and was one of just a handful of cadets chosen to escort President Theodore Roosevelt from the navy side of the stadium to the army side at halftime.

He made it through his second year successfully and was promoted. The most immediate result was that he was now going to be one of those cadets who greeted incoming freshmen for plebe camp. At first he did not like having to be rough on the newcomers, but he quickly adapted to the responsibility, often reporting plebes for any little minor infraction. He was working hard to develop a stern look to use with the underclassmen, no doubt believing that the face of a soldier needed to be tough and serious to the point of a perpetual scowl in order to command respect. He even spent time in front of a mirror, trying to judge how intimidating his scowl looked. The plebes disliked him. He didn't care.

"Always do more than is required of you," he wrote in his journal. "Do your damdest always." He lived up to these strictures and demanded it of everyone. It would be difficult to imagine a cadet who took his responsibilities more seriously than did George Patton. Duty and performance were utmost in his mind and he was intolerant of failure, both his own and that of others. "There is no next time," he said. Whether a football game or a battle, it must be won—it could only be won—the first time. In his letters and journals, he derided himself constantly, scolding himself for not being smart enough and not working hard enough. "Should I fail to do something please cuss me out once in a while," he wrote to Beatrice.

It was clear that Patton was thinking more and more like an army officer. He began to keep a separate notebook just for military musings. Its entries reflected both the knowledge that he gained about the profession of arms and how his own personal tendencies manifested themselves in that profession. One of the central themes to which he always anchored his ideas was *action*: being energetic, relentless, always pushing forward. It was the way he played football. He ran track and set an academy record in the 220-yard hurdles. He soon developed a love of polo for much the same reason (plus it involved horses, which he had loved since childhood). The cavalry, therefore, interested him a great deal. More than any other branch of the army, it embodied this racing energy on the battlefield. Indomitable courage and a quick perception of [the] right moment to attack were characteristics of the bold cavalry leader. Action even dictated the way he took part in drill, accounting for his unequaled soldierly bearing. His journal entry "always do more than is required of you" was not just an empty phrase he wrote. It was the way he thought. In itself, it demanded action. "Always *do* more," he said. As the opposite of doing more, of course, was doing less, those who didn't do more did less. He knew that such a trait, especially in a soldier, could not be tolerated. Hazing by upperclassmen, as long as it did not injure a cadet, was suitable if it corrected or checked the development of such a trait. "In fact lots of them [new cadets] require just such treatment to make them wake up and find themselves," he said. A reason or an excuse for falling short did not matter. It *could not* matter in Patton's view. This intolerance would be a central theme in the way he lived his life, and its consequences, while in the long term usually beneficial, in the short term sometimes caused him no end of trouble and even had the potential to ruin all that he tried to make of himself.

Intellectually, too, Patton was beginning to apply his natural abilities to the practical study of being a good soldier. Since his earliest days of his father and Aunt Nannie reading to him, he had been steeped in history, especially that of combat and war. Even in the Bible there was military history. When he was 15 and 16, he wrote essays about the military exploits of Julius Caesar, Alexander, and Miltiades. He had always excelled at it, but did not seem to realize it. "I can't to save my life care about studies," he wrote to his father, "and even if I did care about them I have not got the head for them. I can not sit down and study," he admitted. But he could and he did—if the topic was military history. He lamented to Beatrice that even if it were peeling potatoes, he would like to find one thing he could do better than anyone else. He saw nothing that he did well. "I am not even an expert potato peeler."

It is difficult, though, to classify knowing history as an ability particularly if one is conditioned to equate abilities with what then-President Theodore Roosevelt so vocally praised as "the strenuous life." Those who can study, remember and internalize its stories and messages, often do so without even knowing that that is what they are doing. Roosevelt had this ability as well; he was equally interested and informed by history's lessons. There is even a certain amount of daydreaming that goes along with contemplative activity, although serious students would be loath to admit it. Rarely is it ever really an active pursuit, so it ran up against Patton's natural inclination for action. But in Patton, sedentary history study somehow shared top billing with nonstop, bone-jarring action. From back before the time he entered VMI, those around him saw it. His stepgrandfather had seen a "strongly developed taste for military history" in the boy and had earnestly pointed it out in a letter to Senator Bard.

At West Point he began to apply his love of military history. He felt like not enough people appreciated it. Even among his fellow cadets there were "comparatively few men in the corps who realize the importance of military study and military history, which is as Napoleon says, the only school of war." He began to collect books on the topic avidly, and would do so all his life. Over the course of his years, Patton's collection of books on military history would grow to almost 500 volumes; most of them completely marked up with notes in the margins and the endpapers. He read the classics, Shakespeare, famous books by military commanders and theorists, biographies, and memoirs. He would develop an appreciation for reading books that either provided a parallel to whatever situation or military problem happened to be facing him at the time, or dealt with the same terrain and region over which he was attacking. Patton came to believe that a thoroughgoing knowledge of history was the only element a commander could call upon to find parallels to whatever situation might be at hand. The mind of a commander would grow with the study of military history to the point at which "he can grasp without effort" the toughest questions in the science of war. Experiences in war, he thought, were the same, whether the year was 1909, 1099, or 399 B.C. No matter when, they were all equally alive to him. Because of these convictions and despite the problems he had studying, Patton would make himself into one of the best-educated and widely read leaders in the entire American army.

Shortly before he graduated, his class went down to Gettysburg, Pennsylvania to visit the battlefield. One evening after dinner he walked out alone through the vast cemetery "and let the spirits of the dead thousands laid there in ordered rows sink deep into me." He crossed through the cemetery, went out its southeastern gate, and wandered out across the Taneytown Road to Cemetery Ridge. Monuments interspersed with cannon meandered southward down the ridgeline. A low stone wall marked the western edge of the ridge, and Patton, lost in thought and imagination, walked over and sat down. Before him stretched a broad shallow valley about a mile wide over to the tree line on the next ridge. Across this field came the disastrous Confederate advance known as Pickett's Charge and commanding the Seventh Virginia Regiment of Kemper's Brigade was his great-uncle Waller Tazewell Patton. George Patton watched as the setting sun turned the sky orange and red as the valley below slipped into darkness. "I could almost see them coming," he wrote Beatrice when he returned to his hotel room: a long line of 14,000 gray-clad soldiers advancing under the guns of the Union army, falling by the dozens, and then hundreds, steadily coming closer to the top of the ridge. None came farther than the men of the Seventh Virginia, led by Patton's uncle. Tazewell had jumped up on the very wall in front of George and had fallen instantly, mortally wounded. He could see them all now, dead in the field, slumped by the wall, fallen in the ranks in which they came, giving their last full measure of devotion. The sense of bravery, duty, and honor was almost overwhelming. Just then Patton heard a quail calling some-where off in the trees and it broke through the roar of the guns in his head. It was a peaceful sound. Not a living soul bothered him as he sat, drinking in the thick emotions of the quiet field. He began to sense that somewhere there was a field like this one that held a special destiny for him, too.

Chapter 4

ADVANCING IN A CAREER

Perhaps by future hidden
Some greatness waits in store
If so, the hopes your praise to gain
Shall make my efforts more.

George S. Patton, Jr. graduated from West Point on June 11, 1909, and was commissioned a Second Lieutenant. He was twenty-three years old and ranked 46 in his class of 103, no small triumph in the face of the troubles he experienced learning and the late start he had in his formal education. He had earned a letter in track and field, was classified as an Expert Rifleman for his work on the rifle range, and was highly regarded for his swordsmanship. His father, mother, Aunt Nannie, and of course, Beatrice were there to cheer him on at the ceremony. It was a warm day and President Taft's Secretary of War Jacob Dickinson was there to give the main address. Afterwards, the class traveled down to New York City by train for the cadet banquet at the Hotel Astor, and the next day, his parents and aunt bought him a stylish watch and chain from Tiffany and Co. as a graduation gift.

A graduating cadet has the opportunity of selecting which branch of the army to join: infantry, artillery, or cavalry. By temperament and interest Patton was best suited for the cavalry. He loved horses, he loved action and speed, always wanted to take the offensive, and he loved the dash and flair of the cavalry. Before graduation he had sought out the advice of Captain Charles Summerall, a professor of tactics who would remain one of Patton's close friends in future years, and Summerall suggested cavalry without hesitation. He knew Patton and his attitudes, plus there was just more to do in the cavalry, he said. It was less likely that a man would get bored. In terms of where he might be stationed, choosing cavalry opened up at least the possibility of being posted to Fort Myer, Virginia, head-quarters of the Fifteenth Cavalry Regiment and right across the Potomac from Washington, D.C. There could be no better place for an ambitious and able young officer and Patton knew he could make great connections with countless higher-ranking officers and within the social circles of the nation's capital.

Another part of the Fifteenth, however, was stationed at Fort Sheridan, Illinois, near Chicago, and that is where freshly minted Second Lieu-tenant George S. Patton, Jr. was sent. After a summer vacation visit to California, he reported for duty in September and found his quarters to be two large, empty, dirty rooms containing a rather pretty mahogany desk and an iron bed. That the rooms had not yet been cleaned and that the man assigned to be his orderly had not yet appeared bothered him. His first morning on the post Patton drank coffee in the mess hall, and then Captain Francis Marshall—the commanding officer of Patton's K Troop—showed him around on an inspection. He had much to learn and Captain Marshall proved to be an ideal teacher for Patton's first duty as-signment. Eventually Patton's missing orderly appeared with two horses and fetched his trunks from the railroad station.

Slowly over the next month, he got more furniture and, of course, more responsibilities. He commanded practice marches and camp setups, regu-larly oversaw the stables, and took target practice, discovering to his relief that not only was he still a crack shot with the rifle but he was also the best pistol shot on the post. He was surprised at the overall ignorance of the average enlisted man, but they struck him as very respectful and, for the most part, hardworking. In his spare time, he and a fellow officer laid out a polo field and four afternoons a week began studying military history, tactics, and strategy together. Surprisingly enough, he had an active social life, but such was relatively normal for young, single army officers near a big city like Chicago. Occasionally Patton went to a football game in Chicago. If a particular play struck his fancy, he would diagram it and send it to the West Point football coach. He went out to the theater and to din-ner often. He missed Beatrice, though, and his job soon grew tedious and boring. "God but I wish there would be a war," he wrote to her. The tiny peacetime army, underfunded and ignored as it was, was looking like a dead-end job.

Patton spent much of the Christmas holiday with Beatrice and her family in Massachusetts. They were very much in love with each other by this time, and began to discuss marriage seriously. Beatrice was hesitant but she truly loved George and soon agreed to be his bride. Her father, however, was flat-out opposed. The two eventually decided rather unchivalrously, that Beatrice, instead of Patton himself, would break the news to Mr. Ayer. When he refused to give his approval, Beatrice locked herself in her bedroom and refused to change her mind. After a week of this, her father relented. "I know your accommodations are not what you would have them in private life," he wrote to Patton after giving in to his daughter, but he knew that "Beatrice enjoys roughing it to some extent, as all good sailors and soldiers must; and you know she is a pretty good sailor." He also informed Patton of his custom to provide each of his married children a secure monthly income and that, despite his initial reluctance, Beatrice would be no exception. No doubt this was a relief to everyone involved especially Patton himself. They were married in an Episcopal church close by the Ayer family estate on May 26, 1910. Beatrice cut the wedding cake with Patton's sword. They honeymooned in England for most of June and then the couple returned together to Fort Sheridan. Just over nine months later, in March 1911, they welcomed their first child, a girl whom they named Beatrice.

The question of how a person advances in a career is a tricky one. The opposite ends of possibility are advancing solely on merit and ability; and, conversely, advancing solely because of whom one knows and by personal connections. Those who do advance in their careers usually tend to believe merit is the determining factor. On the other hand, those who labor diligently, in their impression, and yet never advance tend instead to believe the question rests (unfairly, of course) just on who one knows. In truth, most professional advancement is a combination of these factors, with a little bit of being at the right place at the right time thrown in. For George Patton out at Fort Sheridan, there was a combination of factors at work.

In the spring of 1911, Patton had acted as temporary commander of Troop K, a rare honor for a junior officer like himself. Obviously he was doing well and being noticed. In addition to this, one of his sister-in-law's boyfriends was a well-connected army officer in the capital, and Patton yearned for a transfer to Fort Myer. Exactly how it came about is unclear as to whether or not any extra influence played a role, but in the fall of 1911, Patton was reassigned to the other part of the Fifteenth Cavalry Regiment at Fort Myer.

The officers stationed at Fort Myer came from some of the best families in the nation and took part in countless social activities, from official funerals to state ceremonies. They escorted visiting dignitaries, received invitations to all the fancy balls and dances in the city and its suburbs, and were familiar to all the highest-ranking officers who ran the war depart-ment and the army. The army chief of staff, in fact, lived at Fort Myer. Al-most any officer assigned to duty at Fort Myer would come in contact with the nation's most influential leaders. George Patton certainly intended to use these opportunities in every way possible to advance his career. He was thrilled to be there and at first, he felt like he was at the center of ev-erything. On one of his first days in town, he had lunch with his old friend and professor Charles Summerall from West Point. He immediately struck his new commanding officer, Captain Julian Lindsey, as excellent in ap-pearance, bearing, and professional enthusiasm.

Fort Myer was a terrific place for a passionate horseman like Patton. He loved nothing better than to go for rides on the many trails that criss-crossed the post and quickly fell into a daily routine of doing so. One morning while riding, he happened across the new Secretary of War, Henry L. Stimson, an avid horseman also. Patton impressed Stimson and the two quickly became fast friends and riding partners. Sometimes Stim-son called on Patton to be his aide at social events at Fort Myer and in later years he would help Patton immeasurably. Given Patton's drive to make himself noticed for his energy and his abilities, it was hardly surpris-ing that it took him no time at all to become well-known in all the mili-tary circles within official Washington.

As Patton's horsemanship and athletic ability impressed most everyone around him, he soon became a leader on Fort Myer's polo team and was generally regarded as a very good athlete. When word went around that the International Olympic Games were introducing the modern pen-tathlon as a new medal event and that the competition would be open only to military contestants from participating nations, army officials in Washington knew that Patton was their best choice. The elements of the pentathlon included running, swimming, horseback riding, shooting, and fencing. An event more tailor-made for Patton's abilities could hardly be imagined. He was named to the team in May 1912, and immediately set out for Stockholm, Sweden, the site of the fifth modern Olympics in June.

At Stockholm, Patton performed well. Ironically enough, it was his performance in pistol shooting that probably kept him from a medal. He missed the target completely. In later years, as the story circulated, the as-sumption grew that he simply could *not* have missed the target. A rumor grew that the bullet that *apparently* missed the target must have passed through a hole made by a previous bullet. In reality, however, two of his shots missed. Nevertheless he still scored 169 out of a possible 200 points, but this was low enough to keep him from a medal. He did well in all the other events. He exerted himself to the point of utter exhaustion in the running and swimming, and his bold, charge-ahead style made him a crowd favorite in the fencing competition. He finished fifth in the overall standings. It was a great accomplishment, but back in the states, news of his performance was overshadowed by the success of Native American track and field star Jim Thorpe, who became the first man to win the modern decathlon.

Before Patton headed back to the United States, he stopped over in Saumur, France, home of the French Army's cavalry school, to study swordsmanship for two weeks with that country's premier instructor, Adjutant M. Clery, widely regarded as the best swordsman in the French army. The time flew by, of course, and just three months after he left Fort Myer, he was back.

When Patton returned home, things were a bit different. He was the talk of the town and everyone wanted to hear stories from the Olympics and about his time in France. Many higher-ranking officers, especially, were eager for details. He had dinner with Army Chief of Staff, Major General Leonard Wood, and his old riding friend Henry Stimson, just to give them a personal briefing on every aspect of his recent adventures. Wood soon began to join him for morning rides. Patton wrote up reports—which Beatrice edited for him—of his experiences in Stockholm and Saumur, one of which ultimately appeared as an article in the widely read *Army and Navy Journal*. In Woodrow Wilson's inaugural parade in 1913, Patton rode in a car as General Wood's aide. Later that year, he even helped redesign the standard-issue cavalry saber that soon was widely known simply as the "Patton sword." He was getting exactly what he wanted: noticed. His star was beginning to rise.

His tour of duty at Fort Myer, however, was ending, and he knew that despite the connections he was making, he would soon be transferred elsewhere. He and Beatrice had certainly enjoyed their time there, though, and it would be tough to leave. The social scene of Washington was far more amenable to Bea's tastes than frontier posts, and Patton had been able to ride in horse races from Baltimore to Belmont Park in New York, attend Army-Navy football games, and even gain membership in the capital's exclusive Metropolitan Club. But he also knew that any up-and-coming young cavalry officer had to go through what was then called Mounted Service School at Fort Riley, Kansas. He soon found out that was to be his next stop.

Early in the summer, the orders came assigning him to Fort Riley. Less expected was the order authorizing him to return first to Saumur, France, for a second summer of swordsmanship study. He would have to do so at his own expense, however. Only the wealth of Beatrice's family made such a trip possible. Patton and Beatrice even shipped their automobile over to France so they could use it while they were there. During this stay Patton concentrated as much on teaching techniques as he did on fencing, and also spent a good deal of time touring around the farms and fields of northern France, following in the footsteps of Julius Caesar's legions. He got to know the region called Normandy well, with its distinctive hedgerows that separated the farm fields and pastures and its sunken roads that ran alongside the high hedges. This familiarity would come in very handy in the future when he had to lead soldiers over this same ground. He also attended classes at the French version of the mounted service school and studied military history with Lieutenant Jean Houdemon, like Patton, a rising star in the French Army.

Back at Fort Riley, Patton once again found himself at a frontier post without much in the way of modern amenities. The order and discipline evident on the post, however, was unequalled. Classes in the mounted service school were every Monday through Friday, and in addition to the classes in which he was a student, Patton taught three classes of swordsmanship. Many of his students outranked him. All in all, he told his father, this was "the most strictly army place I have ever been in and also the most strictly business."

Not only did Patton complete two years of mounted service school during his time at Fort Riley; he also turned himself into the army's leading expert on swordsmanship. He also had begun reading military history with a dedication and energy he never before demonstrated. Sometimes he read for as much as twelve hours a day, absorbing the experiences of the past—the lessons of the past—to the limit of his ability. The "more I read," he said, "the more I see the necessity of reading."

By the time Patton was finished at Riley, a torrent of international events had completely changed the world. In the summer of 1914, World War I exploded in Europe, engulfing all the major powers of the continent. President Woodrow Wilson announced that the United States would remain neutral in the war. Nevertheless, Patton wanted in on it. He wrote to General Wood essentially asking permission to go to France and fight alongside his friends in the French army. He even said he would pay his own expenses. Don't even think about it, Wood responded. "We don't want to waste youngsters of your sort in the service of foreign nations," he said. He confided to Patton that he, too, felt the draw to action. "I am also required to look on with patience, but hope to get over at some later time."

Many in the United States, including former President Theodore Roosevelt, became convinced, either at the very outset of the war or as the years went by, that the nation would eventually have to take part. For men like Patton, Leonard Wood, and others who had devoted their life to the study of battle and the professional of arms, sitting on the sidelines was sometimes truly difficult. Very soon, however, Patton found himself in combat and even became the first American soldier to ride into the fight in a motorized vehicle. Such a distinction would not come on the fields of France, at least, not yet. Patton's immediate future lay to the south, across the Rio Grande, in the deserts of Northern Mexico.

Chapter 5

A SOUTHERN ADVENTURE

For victory, apart from you,
Would be an empty gain
A laurel crown you could not share
Would be reward in vain.

In 1915, following his successes at Fort Riley, Patton was transferred to the Eighth Cavalry Regiment, fresh from duty in the Philippines. The transfer kept Patton from shipping out to the Philippines himself, for his regiment was scheduled to replace the troops who were now heading home from the islands. Headquarters for the Eighth Cavalry was Fort Bliss, near El Paso, Texas, and it had suddenly become a hot spot for the American army.

In the years after 1910, Mexico was increasingly torn by instability and civil war. Revolutionaries of one stripe or another overthrew dictators and presidents. The Wilson administration bungled its way into a brief military intervention at Vera Cruz and then, through its recognition of the new administration of Venustiano Carranza, it enraged former Carranza supporter and notoriously violent renegade Francisco "Pancho" Villa. The American government was extremely worried about cross-border incursions by Mexican revolutionaries, and, since Fort Bliss was the post closest to the area of greatest concern, its troops were responsible for patrolling the border.

Patton arrived at the post before the rest of his regiment made it back from the Philippines. Consequently, he had little to do until they arrived.

He spent a lot of time studying for his promotion exam to first lieutenant. He explored the area and examined the buildings on the base. The wooden stables he thought were firetraps even though they, like many of the buildings, were new. He helped a captain train polo ponies although he had little expectations for any high-quality games. Most of the men had never played before.

Finally the officers and men of his new regiment began arriving from the Philippines. Once things at the post settled down, Patton began spending much of his time with detachments of cavalry on patrol out at the numerous remote border outposts along the Rio Grande. The center of his operations was the tiny town of Sierra Blanca, about 90 miles southeast of El Paso and close by the important main line of the Southern Pacific railroad. He hoped that he would be put in command of one of the cavalry troops that ventured out from Sierra Blanca in search of border incursions, local bandit gangs, or any suspicious activity.

While he was out on patrol, accommodations were rough, to say the least. "It may be fine to die with one's boots on," he complained, "but it is very hard on the feet to sleep with them on which is what I have been doing up to last night." Patton was fascinated, however, by the characters he came across in Sierra Blanca. "It is supposed to be very tough," he wrote to Beatrice, "and at least half the men wear boots and spurs and carry guns." Although he thought the country was the most desolate imaginable, "I would not miss this for the world. I guess there are few places like it left." On most patrols there was little action beyond some good hunting. Quail, rabbits, and deer abounded. Once while trotting along on his horse, Patton shot a running jackrabbit from 30 feet with his pistol. It was a great shot. "My reputation as a gun man is made," he said proudly.

Because he would not be able to get time off at Christmas, Beatrice came to Texas to spend the holidays with Patton. She spent December and most of January in Texas. Much to the surprise of the entire family, especially after she broke down in tears during a raging windstorm while visiting Patton in Sierra Blanca and begged him to quit the army, Beatrice found that she actually liked Fort Bliss and El Paso. Consequently, Patton requested officer's quarters on the post, and Beatrice brought the family down, which now included a second daughter, Ruth Ellen. Life for the Patton's took on a semblance of normality. Once again, George played polo and hunted, and once again his wife charmed other officers, their wives, and assorted other personnel on the post. Occasionally Patton's sister Nita would even pay a visit to El Paso, and it was during one of these times that she was introduced to Patton's superior and commanding officer of Fort Bliss, General John Pershing.

In 1915, John J. Pershing was one of the most respected officers in the army, but his time at Fort Bliss started off with an unimaginable tragedy. His wife and their three daughters died in a house fire shortly before they were to join him in Texas. He was crushed. Even though months later he was still numb with grief, Pershing and Nita felt an undeniable attraction to one another the first time they met. He was 55; she was 29 and never married. Before anything like a relationship could take hold, though, things began to change.

Late in 1915 and into 1916, Pancho Villa raided several American border towns, culminating with a raid on Columbus, New Mexico, in which he and his band killed 17 Americans. Wilson vowed action and soldiers from Fort Bliss in far west Texas mounted an expedition to find Villa and end his ability to attack the United States. Pershing received notification that he would be leading the thousands of troops into the Mexican interior to carry out the mission. Nita and Pershing stayed in close touch, though, and before long were in love. For his part, Patton fully intended to be in on the action.

To his irritation, however, Patton's regiment was not among the forces selected for the expedition. Pershing demanded that the soldiers for the operation be in top physical condition and the Eighth Regiment's commander was quite overweight. "There ought to be a law killing fat colonels on sight," he groused bitterly, but he determined to figure out some other way to go with Pershing into Mexico. Finally he wrangled an appointment as a temporary aide when one of Pershing's regular aides was unable to join the group until later.

As Pershing's aide, Patton spent a great deal of time with the general and Pershing's influence on the young lieutenant was close to immeasurable. The two shared the same sense of duty and honor, the importance of training, and even were of like mind when it came to everything from leadership to personal appearance. No frost or snow prevented Pershing's daily shave, Patton observed. He grew to see that the tougher the work his soldiers had to face, the more important little things like this became. Especially in the field of battle, "the sight of a clean, well-shaved officer" was an inspiration to the men. Like his commander, Patton also made it a point always to wear a tie with his uniform, even in the heat when most other officers were wearing open collars. Both men were extremely detail oriented, especially in inspections. "Nothing is too minute to escape Pershing," Patton noted. "A button a shirt not fastened a loose spur" everything had to be just so. "It is this personal care which gets the results," Patton said, "and only this personal care will." He would make it his own philosophy throughout the rest of his career.

The Punitive Expedition, as the operation against Villa came to be known, was made up of a hodge-podge of equipment, both traditional and modern. There were nine regiments of cavalry and one of mounted artillery. Eventually there would be four motor vehicles and even some airplanes for scouting. In many ways, it was groundbreaking for the U.S. Army, and it was somehow fitting that in the middle of such a transformative operation was George Patton. With 7,500 men proceeding along in three separate columns, it was the largest single American military action since the Civil War. More importantly, it was the first time that the army had used automobiles and airplanes, both of which fascinated Patton, alongside its horses and foot soldiers.

Even with all the high-tech hardware, though, Patton never lost his love for horses and cavalry. In its spare time, of which there was much, the expedition staged mock battles, maneuvers, attacks, and cavalry charges. There were machine gun drills and pistol practice. And there were long, interminable treks through the rough and arid Mexico mountains.

Much of the time was taken up by fruitless searching, although the use of airplanes and automobiles created a certain level of interest in and of itself. Real action, however, was rare. Pershing doubted that Villa would dare fight in the open in a traditional battle, and quietly dreaded the notion of a protracted guerilla war. Again, it was somehow fitting that Patton found himself right in the middle of the single most daring and dangerous exchange of the entire mission, and in doing so, gained at least temporary fame.

In May 1916, Pershing sent Patton with three automobiles and ten men to purchase some corn from a nearby ranch. While doing this the party came across one of Villa's subordinates, General Julio Cardenas, and several of his underlings at a remote hacienda near the village of San Miguelito. Armed with a pistol and a rifle, Patton jumped from his car to secure the area. Almost immediately three armed men on horseback appeared and began shooting. Bullets kicked up dirt and pebbles around his feet as a chaotic gunfight broke out. By the time the shooting stopped, Patton and the other soldiers had killed Cardenas and two of his underlings. During a lull in the fighting, Patton had the three bodies strapped to the hood of one of the cars. Then, seeing upwards of fifty horsemen racing toward his position, he quickly ordered the party back into the vehicles and they raced back to the American camp. Soon American newspapers were emblazoned with Patton's photograph, usually one of him calmly smoking a pipe. His actions had turned him into a nationwide sensation. Stories reported the gunfight in dramatic detail. Patton became known as the "Bandit Killer."

For the rest of the year, however, there was little other action for the expedition. For Patton, the growing boredom of what amounted to little more than garrison duty was interrupted only by getting severely burned on his head and hands by the gasoline lamp in his tent. For two painful weeks he was swathed in bandages and spent some sick-leave time in California. Soon, though, he was back in the Mexican desert.

While he diligently kept up his journal, the entries indicated that any other action was rare. One day he wrote nothing except that he trapped a chipmunk. Another day he wrote a memo for Pershing on the proper feeding of horses. "We are all rapidly going crazy from lack of occupation," he wrote. Such was the intensity of his disappointed boredom that at one point he even considered, albeit very briefly, leaving the army. Whether he was really serious or not was another matter. In times of depression both in Mexico and later, Patton would always talk of drastic measures like retirement. He never followed through, of course.

His monotonous days were filled with little but cavalry exercises and mock charges, rifle and pistol practice, and writing reports, letters, and when he was particularly glum, poetry. The nagging doubts that had been so pervasive in his younger years began to creep back. Behind the soldierly bearing he labored so hard to maintain, he had the same uncertainties that everyone else felt. At times he was certain that he would someday be a success, but at other times doubted it would ever be possible. For Patton as for all of us, the not knowing made it all seem like a gamble sometimes. "If I knew that I would never be famous," he said, "I would settle down and raise horses and have a good time." But he knew—at least he often felt he knew—he had greatness before him. And he seemed always to be aware of exactly what his staying in the army was costing him and his family. At times he expressed it with striking honesty. "I wish I was less ambitious," he told Beatrice candidly. "It is a great gamble to your and my own happiness for the hope of greatness."

During these days of boredom, however, Patton began to realize something about the American army. As the World War dragged on and on in Europe, and as it became more likely that at some point the United States would get involved, there was much talk in official Washington circles about preparedness. Despite President Wilson's pronouncements that the United States army was in good shape, from what Patton could see, the army was as far from a state of readiness as could be imagined. The reality he saw around him was not the ideal of which politicians spoke. Knowing the conditions on the battlefields of Europe, he could see that the American army was nowhere near the level it would take to get involved. Part of his sullen attitude, however, probably came from frustration and boredom.

The time he had on his hands, however, he used for reflection. In doing so, the military ideas that he would carry with him for the rest of his life, and so distinguish his future actions as a commander began to take form. One of his biggest projects while in Mexico was a lengthy article he wrote on the expedition's employment of cavalry that would appear early in 1917 in the pages of *Cavalry Journal*. As much as it told of the expedition's activities, it also revealed many of Patton's own ideas about the use of cavalry, and more broadly, the essential nature of movement and maneuver in warfare. His ideas were beginning to come into sharper focus. Even though he would always love horses, he experienced firsthand and began to appreciate the tactical abilities of the automobile. Although it had seemed like a minor issue at the time, George Patton had been the first U.S. Army officer to ride a motor vehicle into combat when he stormed the ranch near San Miguelito. The mobility and speed that cars seemed to offer the military had the potential to exceed even that of horse cavalry.

Cavalry, whether made up of horses or automobiles, had the responsibility of being the army's eyes. It had to push out ahead aggressively and find the enemy. Under no circumstances should it "poke along like Infantry must until it bumps its nose," he said. Of course cavalry had better be able to fight, too. Given the stalemate into which the European war had fallen, it was more important than ever "to have troops that are able to move rapidly from one place to another over any kind of country and arrive at the point of action fit for a fight." He was probably thinking primarily of horses when he wrote this, but the war in Europe, now grinding into its third year, was transforming every idea about the way in which wars were fought.

The time was fast approaching when the U.S. Army would be introduced with shocking suddenness to these changes. Patton would be in the front lines, literally, to witness them. "I have learned more useful soldiering while in Mexico than all the rest of my service put together," Patton said shortly before the expedition returned to the States and what he had learned set him up for what was his next role. He did not know for sure at the time, but George Patton had been on hand when the role of the horse began to wane and motorized vehicles began to replace them. He had seen how they could perform the same functions. American participation in World War I would put these lessons to the test.

Chapter 6

WORLD WAR I

What painted glass can lovelier shadows cast
Than those the Western skys shall ever shed,
While mingled with its light, Red Battle's Sun
Completes in magic colors o'er our dead
The flag for which they died.

In the spring of 1917, the United States finally entered World War I to fight alongside Great Britain and France against Germany and Austria. To justify American sons and fathers going into battle, President Wilson believed that there had to be a greater cause to serve beyond the quarrels and rivalries that had apparently triggered the war in the first place. Accordingly, he had idealistically cast American participation in the conflict as a crusade to reform the way nations dealt with each other. The United States would be fighting to end war as a tool of national power. For Americans, it was now a war, said Wilson, "to end all wars."

The American Army had a long way to go before it would be ready to fight in a conflict as large and as far away as the world war. The total strength of the army in April 1917 was less than 135,000 officers and men, slightly higher if you figured in the National Guard and Reserves. Compared to what was going on in Europe, those numbers were utterly inadequate. On just one single day at the outset of the Battle of the Somme in 1916, the British army had suffered almost half that many casualties. There were not enough weapons, not enough bullets or artillery shells, not enough uniforms, not enough vehicles, not enough horses, not enough of anything for the United States to be able to enter the fighting quickly.

It almost went without saying that mobilizing, supplying, and training the American Army would be a herculean task that would strain the abilities of any military leader. It was up to Wilson's Secretary of War, Newton Baker, to pick the one man to lead this endeavor. There was only one name he seriously considered for the job: John J. Pershing. The way Pershing had handled the Punitive Expedition into Mexico had brought him to the attention of official Washington and the war department and they were impressed with his bearing, his abilities, his organizational skills, and his sense of duty. He was 56 years old, he held the rank of major general, and he seemed to be every bit the model soldier. The war department allowed him to organize what would be called the American Expeditionary Force (AEF) in any way he saw fit. He had a blank check, but he was also starting from scratch. He had a tough job ahead of him.

Meanwhile, George S. Patton was once again stationed at Fort Bliss in far west Texas. He had been given command of Troop A of the Seventh Cavalry Regiment, both a distinct honor and a big responsibility for a new first lieutenant. It was usually considered to be a captain's job, and that he received it at all indicates just how much his superiors thought of his abilities. Soon he was rated an excellent troop commander. He stayed busy writing another article for *Cavalry Journal* and studying for—and passing—the examination for promotion to captain.

All was not good news, though. Both Beatrice's father and mother fell seriously ill at their home in Massachusetts, and as she tended to them, Beatrice herself became sick. Patton traveled north to be whatever help he could, but his abilities as a calm and comforting nurse left much to be desired. All the time he was there, he tried to stay close to the ever-changing situation down in Washington as well.

His connections again paid off. On May 18, Patton received a telegram ordering him to report to the capital at once. His name was on the short list Pershing had drawn up for his headquarters staff. Beatrice was well enough to travel, and her parents were apparently well enough for her to leave them, and the two boarded a train for Washington. When they arrived, they found that Pershing and his staff, and that meant Patton, would be setting sail for Europe in just a matter of days. There was precious little time for all that needed to be done. Even most of his uniforms were still at his quarters out at Fort Bliss. He soon received two more bits of news: first of all, his promotion to captain came through; secondly, as a newly-minted captain on Pershing's staff, he would be supervising all of the enlisted men of the headquarters. He threw himself into the work, which was admittedly rather mundane, but at least he knew he was close to the center of the action, and that made everything worth it.

There was much sorrow as the day of departure arrived. Patton's father, mother, sister, and aunt had all come east to see him off. His sister felt bitter sorrow of her own to see Pershing ship out, for their relationship had blossomed into love over the previous few years. In fact, they were engaged to be married, but had decided to put off doing so until Pershing came back from the war. On a rainy, foggy Monday, May 28, Pershing, Patton, and all the rest of the officers and men of the American Expeditionary Force staff boarded the British steamship *Baltic* for the transatlantic crossing. Numerous delays kept them from a quick departure, but finally, late that afternoon, the coastline of the United States silently disappeared over the western horizon as the *Baltic* headed east for Europe and the war.

The men kept busy aboard the ship. As he would do 25 years later during a similar Atlantic crossing, Patton spent some time studying the culture of where he was headed. Specifically, he and the other men practiced their French. He put in five hours on it every day and soon he was one of the best on the boat, although that "does not speak well for the others," he wrote in his diary. There were lifeboat drills and typhoid inoculations. On the ninth morning out, the men awoke to find that sometime during the night British destroyers had taken up escort positions on each side of the *Baltic* for the last leg of the trip. It was a sudden and serious reminder of the reality of the situation. German U-boats regularly sank allied ships in these very waters, and all aboard were well aware of the danger. The next evening they spotted land and the following morning, a Friday, the ship docked at Liverpool, England. An English band played "The Star-Spangled Banner" and "God Save the King" as the men stood at attention and saluted the flags of the two nations. There were more warm and enthusiastic greetings when they reached London.

While Pershing stayed at the Savoy Hotel, Patton and 67 of his men were quartered at the historic Tower of London. The history and ceremony there impressed Patton greatly. He was told that he and his troops were the first foreign soldiers ever to pass through the gates who were not doing so as prisoners. As he watched the solemn ceremony in which the portals were sealed for the night, a guard informed him that it had happened this way every night for nearly 1,000 years. "Very thrilling," he wrote.

Over the next few days Patton met King George V, the Prime Minister, several generals and admirals and the munitions minister, a forceful man named Winston Churchill. On one evening he went to the theater. Other times there were receptions, banquets, and numerous meetings with their British army counterparts. Wednesday morning at 5:30 a train carrying

Pershing and his staff pulled out of a London station bound for the English Channel. By noon they were in France, met at the port of Boulogne by a detachment of French soldiers. By 6:00 P.M. they were in Paris.

In the French capital the pomp and welcome began afresh. They were again showered with warm and effusive greetings, and once again they were serenaded by "The Star-Spangled Banner." From the train station all the way to their different hotels, the streets were lined with Parisians shouting in celebration and throwing flowers as the small group of American soldiers passed by. Patton stayed at the Hotel Continental, and within four days he was completely exhausted by the welcome they all were receiving. Again he went to the theater and now also to the opera. Again there were banquets and receptions. Again he met a parade of politicians and dignitaries. When he got the time, he practiced his French by reading *The Three Musketeers*. One exciting afternoon, American military aviation pioneer Colonel Billy Mitchell, whom Patton had met back in Mexico, gave him a ride in a biplane. Not once in the first week did he get to bed before midnight. In the midst of all this action, Patton missed his wife terribly. Paris was "a stupid place" without you, he wrote to her, "just as heaven would be under the same conditions."

On Bastille Day he attended a grand parade in which 30,000 French troops marched down the Champs-Elysées. Up until now it had been easy to forget that the most destructive and ghastly war in all of human history was being fought just 60 miles away. But with his soldier's eye, Patton picked out certain details that silently bore witness to the carnage. Out of the thousands of men who marched in front of him that day, he figured he saw fewer than 10 officers pass by who weren't wearing a patch signifying they had been wounded in combat. "Many of them were beardless boys," he soberly wrote his wife.

Later that month, Patton finally got closer to the action. He and Pershing rode out to meet the British Commander in Chief, Sir Douglas Haig, at his muddy headquarters somewhere near the front. Haig was struck immediately by Patton's energy and called him a fire-eater. They all discussed how and where Pershing would be setting up his field headquarters and talked about how much training would have to take place once American troops began arriving in great numbers. Generals from both Britain and France had hoped that they would be able to use soldiers from the United States to fill the shrinking ranks in their own divisions. For the most part, Pershing resolutely refused. In these days of a completely segregated army, however, he did acquiesce in their demands to a certain degree. Pershing had the nickname "Black Jack" because earlier in his career he had served in Montana with the all black Tenth Cavalry Regiment, and he knew that black Americans were effective soldiers just like white Americans. As commander of the entire American Expeditionary Force in France, he assigned four black regiments to fight with the French army and they did so with distinction. Ultimately, 40,000 black Americans saw combat in World War I, most of them fighting with French divisions. Over 300 were decorated for bravery under fire.

Pershing had initially left official Washington speechless with his request for one million men by 1918, but the Wilson administration and Congress quickly complied by instituting a Selective Service system. In July, men of the First Infantry Division—the famous "Big Red One" as they became known for their shoulder patch—began to trickle into France. They were the first fighting forces to arrive. Soon it would be a flood, and these men would need training before they could contribute in any way. Pershing insisted that the soldiers of the AEF would live up to West Point standards in terms of behavior, training, and appearance. Pershing was liable to appear at any place at any time to check on his soldiers. Patton was always right behind him. There was little time to lose. The men had to be turned into soldiers and put into action. The demoralized British and French were concerned with numbers above all else, as they expected that in the spring of 1918, Germany would be able to return to the strategic offensive for the first time since 1914.

On September 1, Pershing, Patton, and the staff moved to their new headquarters in the small town of Chaumont, five hours southeast of Paris. The entire region was to be an enormous training area for the American army, and Patton, now in charge of all the enlisted men on the headquarters staff, had more to do than ever before in his life. Most of his work was administrative, however. There were mountains of paperwork and he was always on the phone. "You know how I hate to telephone," he wrote Beatrice in frustration. "Well, I live at the end of one now."

He fought tedium and missed his wife terribly. He also worried almost constantly that he wasn't going to make it into the fighting. Sometimes it was all too much and he became depressed, and when he did so, he fell back into the old habit of doubting his abilities. "I would give a lot to have you consol me and tell me that I amounted to a lot even when I know I don't," he wrote her glumly.

Occasionally Patton found himself near the front lines, and one night he came upon a battlefield still strewn with the bodies of soldiers who had fallen there. It was nearly impossible to tell who was German, who was British, and who was American, he wrote to Beatrice. They all looked so young. He thought of how often their mothers had changed their diapers and wiped their noses. He found the scene almost unbearable. The sooner the allies won the war, he thought, the sooner young men like this wouldn't be lying dead in the mud. It affected him deeply. When he returned to his quarters, he wrote a lengthy mournful poem he titled "The Moon and the Dead."

Amidst the tedium of his staff work, he kept hearing little bits of talk and rumor that caught his attention. In hopes of smashing through the long and costly stalemate on the front, the British army was busily experimenting with mysterious fighting vehicles known elusively as "tanks." The name had been chosen at random to disguise the real purpose of these heavily armored, lumbering vehicles. Should the Germans hear that the British were experimenting with tanks, it would surely arouse no suspicion. These machines, however, had the capacity, at least in theory, to rumble across no-man's-land between the lines, shield their occupants from the hail of machine gun fire, pin the enemy soldiers in place, smash flat the endless coils of barbed wire in front of the trenches, and decisively overrun the German positions. If they worked, they could win the war. Little wonder they were shrouded in secrecy.

Despite the high hopes and the generally successful experiments, there was almost no consensus on how to use them. Should they travel slowly and be used independently of the infantry? Should instead they be faster and lighter, able to maneuver and coordinate attacks with the foot soldiers? The British and the French tended to be on opposite sides of the question, the British favoring the former idea and the French the latter.

Desperate to take any action that could move his career along, Patton worked up the nerve to tell Pershing that he'd like to be re-assigned to work with the French in their tank program. He tried every way he could think of to sell himself as the perfect man for tanks. He had worked with gasoline-powered automobiles since 1905, he told his boss. He spoke French better than 95 percent of American officers. He had quick judgment and was willing to take chances. He even reminded Pershing, in case the general had forgotten the episode in Mexico, that he was the only American "who has ever made an attack in a motor vehicle." It was how he characterized his ideas of fighting, however, that revealed the most about the way he envisioned their use. He was thinking like a cavalryman. "I have always believed in getting close to the enemy," he told Pershing, "and have taught this for two years at the mounted service school where I had success in arousing the aggressive spirit in the students."

Pershing was convinced and Patton got his wish. The day before his birthday in 1917 he became the first American soldier in the new tank corps. He was ordered to the French tank-training center at Chamlieu to gather all the information he could, and then he was to establish the American Tank Corps training center at the ancient Roman walled city of Langres. It would be a fitting scene for such an avid student of military history as George Patton. At Chamlieu he drove a French tank and fired its gun. It thrilled him. He went to the Renault tank factory to see how they were designed and built. His thirst for information was unquenchable and even though he made a pest of himself, his French hosts were impressed by all he wanted to know. He hurried to pick the mind of a British colonel named J. F. C. Fuller who had just participated in the biggest tank attack yet at the battle of Cambrai. If all this new motorized weaponry either fell through, didn't catch on, or wasn't ready in time, he confided to Beatrice, he could always go over to the infantry to see some action, but he sensed the future in the tank. George S. Patton had finally met his perfect weapon.

Because the city had precious little land to spare, Langres proved unsuitable for a tank school and Patton moved a few miles away to the village of Bourg. As he began to set up the American training center, he wrote a 58-page paper on tanks and their use. He envisioned that they would proceed into action alongside heavily armed soldiers and the two would act in support of each other. At most times, he said, the tank should really be thought of as a "heavily armored infantry solider," just more destructive. But the real clue to the way he was thinking was what should happen when a breakthrough occurred. At that point the tanks should become cavalry, relentlessly pursuing the enemy and running him to the ground. Speed, boldness, and action would be of the essence then, just like in the days of the horse cavalry that he so loved but whose day now had passed.

Despite his interest in the tank, Patton was not a soldier who believed that technological advances negated the real key to winning battles: the soldier himself. It would still be the fighting spirit and energy of the soldiers that would make the difference in combat. "Wars may be fought with weapons," he said, "but they are won by men. It is the spirit of the men who follow and the man who leads that gains the victory." Consequently, in training, Patton sought to instill pride, honor, and a driving sense of duty. His behavior as a commander mirrored that of Pershing. He would appear out of nowhere and take the men by surprise with snap inspections. If everything down to the soldiers' uniforms wasn't in topnotch shape, Patton would loudly and profanely set things straight. He insisted on the most rigorous standards of behavior and discipline. "Lack of discipline in war means death or defeat," he warned his men. The troops of Alexander the Great and the Roman Legions were conquerors because of discipline, he explained. "It is by discipline alone that all your efforts, all your patriotism, shall not have been in vain."

In the same way that his grandfather had designed the bright uniforms of the Kanawha Rifleman back in the 1850s, George Patton designed a distinctive patch for the tank corps and a special ornament to be worn on the uniform collar. He wanted his men to feel set apart, to feel distinctive and proud of what they were doing. That pride was almost as important as discipline.

He worked tirelessly getting his men ready for combat. In January 1918, he was promoted to major, and was soon chosen to command the first two tank battalions created. Although it took time to accumulate the tanks, Patton trained the 950 men and officers under him relentlessly, month after month. He only had a few tanks so all of his troops had to train in shifts. At any given time, as many as half of his tanks were broken down and in the maintenance shop. Often he wondered whether or not he'd made the right decision. An infantry regiment he had had a chance to join had already seen battle and that made him jealous. There was no certainty on the other hand that he himself ever would. That thought nagged at him almost daily.

Finally the waiting came to an end. In August he received orders that his tank brigade was to take part in a broad American offensive aimed at reducing the St. Mihiel salient, a fourteen-mile-deep, twenty-four-mile-long bulge in the allied lines that had remained unchanged since 1914. Fifteen American divisions would be joined by five French divisions in the attack. Here on this section of the battlefield, the very front positions were only about half a mile apart at some points and there were regular exchanges of artillery fire and poison gas attacks. Patton would be in command of two battalions using a mix of British and French tanks. Getting everyone and all the equipment into place was a tremendously difficult undertaking. For a while it was up in the air as to whether or not all the tanks would even arrive in time. The last one was unloaded from the train a mere two hours before the offensive was to begin.

Patton took time to write out a final order to his men, urging them on to boldness and rallying their spirits in anticipation of a decisive victory. "No tank is to be surrendered or abandoned to the enemy." If your tank breaks down and you're "left alone in the midst of the enemy," he said, "keep shooting. If your gun is disabled use your pistols and squash the enemy with your tracks.... As long as one tank is able to move it must go forward." Attack, he said, and keep on attacking. It was the way George Patton knew the war must be fought.

At 1:00 A.M., September 12, four hours before the attack began, the artillery opened up on the German lines. The sky lit up like lightning. The ground rumbled and shook. Just then the heavens, too, opened up and the rain began falling in torrents. At 5:00 A.M. the shelling stopped and the tanks and infantry went forward. Through the rain and the fog, Patton watched as his tanks crept across the shallow valley toward the German positions visible in the near distance. His frustrations grew as he watched tank after tank bog down in the front trenches of the German lines. As the attack proceeded, he moved as far forward as he could, almost two miles, stopping only when his telephone wires would reach no further. He was under orders to remain in contact with headquarters, but before him stretched the battlefield and he felt compelled to do all he could in person. By 7:00 he had had enough of waiting and watching and started out on foot to prod the attack forward.

The whole country was alive with tanks, he said later, crawling over trenches and through the woods. Exploding shells had blown deep craters into the muddy ground. In one he found a soldier crouched down whom Patton figured was hiding from the fray. The thought that here was a cowardly soldier shirking his duty while others bravely continued forward made him mad. I "went to cuss him out," he said, intending to rally the man forward, but found instead that the young man had been shot through the head. As he continued on, he discovered that in almost every single shell-hole there were dead and wounded men.

Patton pushed ahead with a lieutenant and four runners to relay communications, and passed through several small villages. His right-hand tank battalion had been instructed to attack the villages of Essey and Pannes, but had proven unable to cross the main trench line, which in some places was up to 14 feet wide. It was approaching 10:00 A.M. when Patton finally made it through the drizzle, fog, mud, and explosions to the edge of Essey. There he came upon some members of the Forty-second Infantry Division, most taking shelter inside shell holes, waiting for the artillery barrage to end. Their commander, Brigadier General Douglas MacArthur, was standing on a little rise, surveying the scene. In the din of the battle, as shells roared overhead and an almost constant rumbling shook the ground, Patton and MacArthur stood together, each more concerned about the job his respective units were trying to do than with what the other man was doing or thinking. They exchanged some small talk, as artillery crashed in the near distance, but each was really too wrapped up in the immediate task at hand to say much. Patton climbed a nearby hill in time to see several German soldiers hastily retreating beyond the town. He quickly asked MacArthur if it was all right for him to proceed on to the town of Pannes, and when the general agreed, Patton pushed on ahead.

Exhausted, Patton, a lieutenant, and one of the runners flagged down one of the tanks and rode along on top of it. Behind them came the infantry. All along the way were dead Germans and horses—most had been killed by the artillery. As they neared Pannes, his companions hopped off the tank to assist in rounding up some prisoners, but Patton rode all the way through the village. Suddenly the sound of a heavy machine gun filled the air and paint chips began flying off the tank just inches below his hand. He leapt from the tank into a nearby shell hole but the machine gun fire followed him. It tore at the muddy edge of the little crater above his head as Patton shrank down as much as he could. Finally the shooting stopped and the remaining Germans fled as more American tanks and infantry begin to file into the town.

All across the battlefield the Americans were moving slowly but steadily toward their objectives. Still, the battle continued for over four days. Even though the German army had decided to pull back to a more easily defended position before the attack began, by the time it wound down, Pershing's soldiers had captured over 16,000 prisoners, almost 450 artillery pieces, and had secured their objectives. Patton received a thorough chewing-out from his commanding officer, who was angry that he had left his command post position that first morning, and felt that, in general, if you were a brigade commander like Patton, you did your work from the rear, not the front. If nothing else, those above you could find you easier. Communications were poor to nonexistent during the war however, and it was unlikely that Patton could have had any effect at all on the fighting from far behind the action and he knew it. In the future, he would try to secure better communications with his superiors, but Patton had no desire to stay behind when he sent his men into action.

From all corners of the battlefield came stories about how the tank corps had performed in the battle. When he heard that one lieutenant in command of a small squad of three tanks had charged, cavalry-style, into a German gun emplacement and captured the gun and routed its crew, Patton was enthused and very impressed. If there had been more tanks at that exact point, he thought, there might have been a chance for a substantial breakthrough. He began to envision a different role for tanks: one based on speed, maneuverability, and decisive actions instead of acting merely as infantry support. Tanks could be massed like heavy cavalry and used to deliver a knockout blow to the enemy. These were ideas, experiences, and lessons upon which he would draw in the future.

Halfway around the world, the Los Angeles newspapers ran a story on the battle of St. Mihiel. The headline read "Californian Perched on Tank During Battle," and sure enough, there in the accompanying picture was southern California's own George Patton atop one of his tanks during the battle. "He loves the tanks," Beatrice wrote of her husband, "they seem to fulfil all his expectations."

While sporadic fighting continued on as the Germans mounted a handful of counterattacks in the St. Mihiel area, the energetic offensive had straightened out the bulge in the line within 36 hours. Patton's tank corps had conducted itself very well, and Patton himself had set an important precedent as a tank commander out in the middle of the action with his tanks and men, not far behind the fighting at some communications point. As he looked back over the battle, however, he found himself disappointed because he felt like German resistance had not been strong enough to really give his men a test. Only two tanks had been lost by direct German artillery fire, 40 had bogged down in the muddy trenches while almost that many had simply run out of gas. Five of his men had been killed. He was not sure that the combat had been tough enough to give him a realistic idea of how strong his force really was.

There was no time to rest now. Patton immediately received orders to move 60 miles northwest to participate in an even bigger battle to be known as the Meuse-Argonne offensive. He and his tanks would be supporting two infantry divisions and attacking where the Aire River flowed through a gap between two large forests, one of which was the deep and dark Argonne forest. That his tanks were moved by rail made things much easier on Patton; thousands of other trucks, troops, horses, and mules turned the roads into rivers of mud.

It rained constantly. But when it didn't rain and the sun came out, the drone of German airplanes hunting for signs of an offensive made Patton continually shift his tanks from place to place. To avoid the fuel supply problems that had slowed many of his tanks in the previous operation, Patton ordered that each tank go into this fight with two big spare gas cans strapped to their backs. At night he crept out beyond the front lines and inspected the ground on which he and his men would soon be fighting. The forest was nearly deserted in the day, he wrote his wife, but "from dark to dawn it is alive with men and horses and guns."

The front line exploded to life early in the foggy morning of September 26. Thousands of guns rained artillery shells down on the German positions. At 5:30 A.M., after three hours of such continual pounding, American troops and tanks went forward. Patton remained at the First Tank Brigade command post for an hour, and then moved forward himself, following in the tracks of his tanks. The fog and smoke made it almost impossible to see more than 10 feet in any direction, he said, but nevertheless he pressed onward with six runners and a compass. Some time around 10:00 the fog began to lift and it became easier to see. Suddenly from every direction, the fire of German machine guns began filling the air. To his shock, Patton found that he had actually passed by most of his tanks in the fog and now was out ahead of everyone in a completely exposed position. He and the men with him ran as hard as they could to take cover in a nearby railway cut.

The situation grew more and more chaotic. Soon there were soldiers everywhere, many of whom had gotten hopelessly lost from their units in the forest and the fog. Some hurriedly dove into the railroad cut with Patton as shells exploded and bullets hissed. Patton discovered that he was the only officer anywhere around, and before long he figured there were several hundred men taking cover with him. A few panicked soldiers started to run, while others fumbled with their gas masks. Through his constant cursing and shouting, Patton at least kept them all together and kept even those who were the most terrified from fleeing to the rear.

As the fog continued to thin and the clouds began to break, Patton and his men again started to hear German spotter airplanes that were now able to go up and provide direction for their artillery. Moments later, shells began exploding frightfully close by. The volume of fire became so heavy and accurate that they simply had to risk moving. Patton quickly led everyone about 100 yards southward to the backside of a small hill. American tanks now began arriving but had slow-going in crossing the defensive trenches the Germans had dug. Patton and his men grabbed shovels from the sides of the tanks and began caving-in the trenches so the tanks could pass. The tanks finally got across and amid yelling, cursing, and beating on the sides of his tanks with a walking stick, Patton began to direct them up the hill and into the teeth of the German machine guns. As the tanks began slowly lumbering up the hillside, an infantry sergeant approached Patton and explained that since none of his officers was around, he had no orders. Patton got up, despite being admittedly terrified, and waved his walking stick in the air and shouted, "Follow me!" They headed up the hill.

Later Patton would relate that in the dark gray clouds swirling above the German positions he saw the faces of his ancestors and he suddenly grew calm. Just then a bullet struck him in the left thigh and tore out through his backside. Patton stumbled about 40 feet and then collapsed. Walking alongside him when he was hit had been a private named Joseph Angelo, who now managed to drag the conscious but gravely wounded Patton into a shell hole and at least slowed down the bleeding. The attack moved on ahead, but of the first six men who had initially jumped up to follow Patton, five were already dead. German soldiers had swung around into the same railroad cut the Americans had earlier evacuated. Patton and Angelo found themselves pinned in the hole. They were trapped and couldn't move. Patton continued to bleed. One of the American tanks stayed close to the hole, however. It reminded Patton of a loyal watchdog.

No one could move until the German soldiers were forced out of their positions. For around two hours, Patton lay in the hole. At some point it occurred to him that were he to live, in just a few weeks he would be turning 33. His grandfather had been 33 when he was killed at the Third Battle of Winchester in 1864. About 1:30 in the afternoon, the Germans were finally pushed back and Angelo could raise his head out of the hole. Soldiers dashed up and carried Patton two miles to the rear on a stretcher. It was "not at all pleasant," he remembered later. He was put on an ambulance but demanded first to be taken by a command post so he could personally report what was going on at the front. He was so forceful, the ambulance driver agreed. After doing so, Patton was at last taken to a makeshift field hospital for emergency surgery and then by train to a larger base hospital.

Several days later, Patton was able to write Beatrice that he was alive and well but "missing half my bottom," and that he had a hole in his hip "about as big as a tea cup" that the doctors had to leave open to drain. Soon, however, he could sit up in a wheelchair, so his doctors let him be wheeled outside where he would smoke his pipe and read. In about a month, he was transferred to a hospital near Langres, where he had started his journey with the tank corps. In short order, the men there realized that being gravely wounded had had no bearing on the way Patton expected the center to run. He issued orders about soldierly appearance, personal cleanliness, and military behavior. It was just like before. He wrote letters recommending several of his men for special awards or medals and other, more difficult letters to the families of his men who had been killed in combat. Both Patton and Joe Angelo received the Distinguished Service Cross for their actions.

The same day George Patton turned 33 years old and got rid of his bandages the war came to an end. He spent a week in Paris and then traveled around eastern France, neighboring Luxembourg, and into parts of Germany. He lectured to generals about his experiences with tanks and even staged attack and maneuvering demonstrations. He was suddenly an authority on tanks. He read hundreds of British, French, German, and American reports and tactical papers, and took his first ride on a horse since being wounded. It "did not hurt my tail too much" and he was encouraged. In January 1919, the month that President Woodrow Wilson arrived in Paris for the peace conference, his plan to create a lasting world peace in hand, Patton was ordered to stand ready to shut down the tank center and move everything to the United States. He and his men packed up and shipped out at the end of February. The adventure of World War I was over. For all he knew, he had fought his big war.

Another transatlantic boat ride later, this one much easier on the nerves, he was stepping onto the docks in Brooklyn, New York. As was becoming regular, the newspapers seemed to be drawn to him. His picture was in the New York papers, and the Los Angeles paper ran stories of Patton's exploits. To his surprise, he was something of a hero. That was fine by him. He was happy to be home and eager to see Beatrice and their children. He was also completely uncertain as to what would be next in the career of a peacetime army officer.

U.S field headquarters near Casas Grandes, Mexico. Patton is fourth from the right. 1916. Courtesy of the Library of Congress.

Major General John J. Pershing, 1917. Courtesy of the Library of Congress.

U.S. Colonel George S. Patton, Jr. during World War I. AP/Wide World Photos.

Major General George S. Patton, Jr., Commander of U.S. Forces in French Morocco, is pictured here at Camp Anfa with Vice Admiral Lord Louis Mountbatten of Great Britain, Chief of Combined Operations, 1943. Courtesy of the Library of Congress.

said. I may return to Feriana. Well it is taking care rather a mess but I will make a go of it. I think I will have more trouble with the British than with the Boches. "God favors the brave," "Victory is to the audacious".

3-5-43

Am leaving in a few minutes for Alger. Hope for the best.

This terminates this volume Gen Keyes will see that it gets to you. It is too frank to be shown any one but may some day be of historical value.

G S Patton Jr.

General Patton's diary entries for March 1943. Courtesy of the Library of Congress.

Lt. General George Patton instructing troops in Sicily, 1943. Courtesy of the Library of Congress.

Patton in action. Courtesy of the Library of Congress.

George Patton in front of tank.
Courtesy of the Library of Congress.

Secretary of War, Robert Patter-
son, places flowers on Patton's
grave, 1946. Courtesy of the
Library of Congress.

Poster for the motion picture, Patton. George C. Scott portrays George Patton, 1970. Courtesy of the Library of Congress.

Chapter 7

WANDERING

I stood in the flag-decked cheering crowd
Where all but I were gay,
And gazing on their extecy,
My heart shrank in dismay.

When he returned to the United States, George Patton found that for the time being, both he and his tank corps were to be stationed at Camp Meade, Maryland, where his official role would be commander of the 304th Brigade. Tanks and their officers who had been training at bases and posts throughout the country were also all reassigned to Meade. Despite his official assignment, Patton spent much of his first months back in Washington, D.C., contributing to a comprehensive report about the role tanks had played in the war. Meanwhile, Beatrice moved to Camp Meade and the whole family was together again under the same roof for the first time since they lived in west Texas.

In the fall of 1919, during his time at Camp Meade, Patton met a young lieutenant colonel from Kansas named Dwight D. Eisenhower. Eisenhower or "Ike" as his friends called him, had graduated from West Point in 1915, but had not been shipped over to Europe during the war. On the contrary, he had been assigned to a tank-training center near Gettysburg, Pennsylvania. Despite their rather distinct personality differences, Patton and Eisenhower quickly took to one another and became fast friends. One thing they had in common was the deep conviction that tanks had the ability to greatly alter the future of warfare.

Over the next 20 years, Patton wrote lengthy papers, read, and talked about tanks incessantly to anyone who would listen. He believed that in order for the tank to become a truly decisive force on the battlefields of the future, it had to remain independent of both the infantry and the cavalry. Its revolutionary potential demanded a revolutionary doctrine for its use. "Like the air service," he wrote perceptively, tanks were "'destined for a separate existence." If tanks were simply appended to any existing force, they would be as useless as "a third leg to a duck." He and Eisenhower spent long evenings, into the wee hours, discussing questions of doctrine and maneuver, and took comfort that they agreed on the revolutionary potential of tanks, even if no one else in the army did. Patton and Ike saw in them the very future of warfare and each published controversial articles along these lines in *Infantry Journal*. Patton even wrote a letter to the Naval War College ambitiously asking them if they could send him all the information they had on how ships maneuvered in battle lines, because he thought that such fighting was the closest parallel to the actual tank-to-tank fights he envisioned in the future.

The army, however, had other thoughts and it did not consult these two young officers for their opinions. On the contrary, official Washington was often annoyed by their rather rebellious attitude and writings. At one point, Eisenhower was called to Washington by the army's chief of infantry to justify some of his and Patton's contentions. Ike was bluntly told that he and Patton should keep their opinions to themselves. They were not to publish "anything incompatible with solid infantry doctrine," under the threat of court-martial. In 1920, the army disbanded the 154 officers and 2,508 men of the tank corps as an independent unit, and assigned all of its equipment, officers, and men to the infantry.

As the army quickly began to shrink to its pre-war levels, most of the wartime commissions expired and men like Patton were set back to the level of rank they held before the country entered the war. By the end of the summer, however, he was promoted back up to major, but Patton had no inclination to transfer to the infantry, which was apparently what was going to happen if he wanted to remain involved with tanks. He was disappointed in the way the army was treating the tank corps, and he felt like he'd simply be happier back at home in the cavalry. He figured perhaps, he could be re-assigned to Fort Myer and once again enjoy the lively social life of Washington. Maybe he could resume his prewar experience as a prominent staff officer. He'd just get back on a horse and try to forget the gasoline, oil, and grease of the tanks. Tanks would languish in the infantry. In the cavalry, there would be no new doctrines or exciting new ideas to explore and test but there would at least be the comfort of long, elite traditions and he'd be with horses again.

The overall mood of the nation, too, shifted the military to the back-burner of the country's attention. Within a few years, the millions of men in arms were all but gone. The Washington Naval Conference provided for American battleships to be scrapped in the name of avoiding another dangerous naval arms race. Congress set the upper limit of the army at 125,000 men and 12,000 officers. The army was in a terrible mess, Patton groused, "and there seems to be no end to it." He was convinced that the precipitous demobilization was a grave mistake, and the apparent attitude of most Americans—that disarmament was the best course to preserve the peace—infuriated him. His sense of the future was amazingly prescient and foreshadowed what would not become a general sense by most Americans until at least 15 years later. "We are like people in a boat floating down the beautiful river of fictitious prosperity and thinking that the moaning of the none too distant waterfall—which is going to engulf us—is but the song of the wind in the trees," he wrote in October 1919. He swallowed his disappointment and disgust and was soon back in the cavalry and stationed at Fort Myer. As if the war had never happened, he was once again giving lectures to new cavalry soldiers on horseshoeing, stable management, and the proper ways to carry out a cavalry charge.

His rank allowed the family to live in a big Victorian house on the post with a beautiful view of Washington. Patton played polo again, and went to horse shows. Beatrice again entertained some of the most prominent figures in official Washington. One of their guests was an especially familiar face but was also a reminder of some of the bitter changes that war always brings. John Pershing's courtship of Patton's sister had fallen apart by the end of the war and the wedding was cancelled. For reasons known only to him, Pershing had begun to distance himself from Nita before he even returned from Europe. There were rumors that he had found someone else. Patton tried to get the two back together but to no avail. Nita returned his wedding ring. Of all the family, only Patton's father was not unhappy. He had never approved of his daughter marrying Pershing anyway and was personally relieved to know the courtship was over. The rest of the Pattons, however, were sad and disappointed.

In years after the war, Pershing would still come around to the Patton's home at Fort Myer for dinner. After the meal, he and Patton would inevitably end the evening by having drinks and talking into the night about their experiences in combat. On one such occasion, Pershing broke down and admitted to George how sad he was that things had not worked out with his sister. He had made a horrible mistake in not marrying Nita back before the war had started, he said through his tears. "Lots of men die in wars," Beatrice would later try to explain to her children when they asked about Pershing, "but some of them who have very strong bodies go on living long after the person inside of them, the real them, is dead. They are dead because they used themselves all up in the war." So it was with the great Black Jack Pershing, architect of the American victory in the Great War. Neither Pershing nor Nita ever married anyone else for the rest of their lives.

As long as the army was going to willfully disregard his recommendations and, along with the general public and most of the politicians, persisted with its head-in-the-sand attitude toward what Patton knew the future would hold, he figured that he would at least go ahead and do all he could to advance his career even if his future was completely uncertain. Consequently, early in 1923 he went west to attend the cavalry school at Fort Riley, Kansas and there completed the advanced course. After spending the summer on leave with Beatrice in Boston, he was off again. Because he had graduated high in his class at Riley, he was eligible to move on to the next stage in an officer's professional education, the Command and General Staff School (C&GSS) at Fort Leavenworth. Back to Kansas he went. Beatrice did not join him there, however. She remained in Boston because she was now expecting their third child.

The work at the C&GSS, as the army called it, was hard and the tough competition for high marks demanded more study than Patton had ever had to do in his life. He excelled at it, though, and graduated with honors. The commandant of the school reported that Patton was one of the "ablest and best officers of his grade in the service." Upon graduation, Patton was assigned to be a staff officer in charge of personnel and mobilization plans for all the reserve units in New England. He would be stationed in Boston. The news thrilled Beatrice, and Patton himself was pleased, too, for he would be able to spend time with the newest member of the family. A boy, little George Smith Patton IV, had been born on Christmas Eve, 1923, while Patton had been back for a short break. Now he would be able to get to know the son for whom he had waited so long.

For Beatrice too, this was the happiest time of their entire married life. But she had learned to understand how life worked when you were the wife of an army officer. She knew it would not last long. Sure enough, before a year went by, Patton was again transferred. He had assumed that his next duty post would probably be Washington, D.C., again. That would be all right. Beatrice and the family could handle that. When Patton's papers came through, however, it was another tremendous surprise. The family was not heading down to Washington. The Pattons were headed for Hawaii.

George Patton went to Hawaii ahead of the family. He sailed from New York to Panama, but unlike his grandmother in 1866, he crossed the isthmus via the Panama Canal instead of having to travel overland. After a quick stopover in San Francisco, he headed west for the Hawaiian Islands. When finally the islands came into view, they reminded him of Catalina Island off the coast of California where he had spent so much happy time as a youngster. He would be working just 21 miles outside of Honolulu at Schofield Barracks, the headquarters of the army's Hawaiian division.

His family soon joined him there and to everyone's relief, Beatrice absolutely loved it. She was completely taken by Hawaiian culture, and wrote a historical novel about the islands and translated several of the native legends into French. Both projects were later published. She even took hula lessons. She and her husband often went dancing and sailing together. There were numerous parties. He played polo at every chance and got himself elected president of a riding club. It was a happy time.

Patton spent just over three years stationed in Hawaii where he served in staff positions as both a personnel officer and an intelligence officer. He arrived in time to take part in the "Grand Joint Army and Navy Exercises" in 1925 and greatly impressed the commander. "His tactical judgment is superior, he is well balanced, and he is a quick and enthusiastic worker." Patton would be "an excellent commander of combat troops during war." Another of his superiors perhaps pointed out the obvious when he said that Patton was better suited for active duty than for the routine of office work. Office work, however, was about all there was at this stage and in this army. But Patton never stopped writing and thinking about how the next war would be fought, and continued to imagine the leading role he would be able to play in it.

When Patton learned that his friend Ike Eisenhower had graduated from the Command and General Staff College at the head of his class, he was delighted. He was especially happy to hear that the notes he had lent to Ike helped him do so well. Now was no time to become complacent and tradition-bound, Patton warned his friend. The two warriors had to keep thinking in revolutionary terms. They had to stay open to new ideas for the army, even though the future was uncertain and they both remained somewhat embittered from the disbanding of the tank corps. "I don't try for approved solutions any more," Patton confided to Eisenhower, "but rather to do what I will do in war."

For his part Patton wrote a great deal and gave lectures on everything from leadership to the ways in which future wars would be fought. Winning would still boil down to the two factors of leadership and of getting overwhelming force of the right sort at the right place at the right time. But more and more Patton seemed interested in the concept of leadership and how, exactly, a leader best did his job. He, Ike, and everybody else still talked and wrote a lot about tactics, but he felt like he was never getting to the central question of how to win a war. What makes a soldier fight? Was it fear? Was it the lure of heroism? Was it honor?

Soldiers fought most of all because of commands from their leaders, Patton was coming to believe. This made it absolutely imperative for leaders to be bold, daring, and courageous and this all came from emotion, not intellect. "The man who would qualify as a leader must lead—lead not by the cold incandescence of his super-refined intellect but by the fiery passion of his blazing manhood," he wrote. If a commander was not out there on the front lines he simply was not leading. The army did not sufficiently emphasize "the necessity for personal exposure and rash boldness on the part of our officers," he said. The elements of a good soldier were indoctrinated by example only—the discipline, the appearance, the behavior—but most of all, the courage. A soldier could get very little inspiration from a "squeaking voice made dim and quavering" by miles of telephone cable.

At the very point of conflict it was the courage of the soldier, not any sort of modern technology, that won the battle. "It is the fierce determination of the driver to close with the enemy, not the mechanical perfection of a Mark VIII tank that conquers the trench." And to spur that determination and to ensure that it was always there was the job of the commander, "not as a disembodied brain linked to his men by lines of wire and waves of ether; but as a living presence, an all pervading visible personality," he believed. It reflected exactly what he had learned on the fields of France. This was the way he himself would command, if he ever again got the chance. A leader must be an actor, he admitted, but a true leader also had to live the part absolutely. A determination to "conquer or perish with honor" was the secret of victory.

Patton knew that almost everyone had fear inside him. Courage meant choking it down and doing your job. Cowardice, fear, hesitation, or in Patton's terms, skulking could not be tolerated for one little instant or it would spread and wipe out all that the leader had instilled by example.

The Hawaiian Islands afforded the army one ability that could not be had out on the plains of Kansas or at Fort Myer on the Potomac. Here the army could practice amphibious operations or attacks from the sea across the beach. Patton supervised training exercises as the commanding general of an attacking force. One mock amphibious scenario stipulated that Pearl Harbor was to be the objective of an attack. Such observation and practice would serve Patton well, for in just under 20 years, he would lead two attacks across a beach into enemy territory.

While stationed in Hawaii, Patton had to face the greatest personal trauma of his life and one that must have haunted his thoughts for at least a few years before this. When the family went home to California for Christmas in 1926, Patton's father had told him that he had tuberculosis, and that it had settled in his kidneys. It was a serious case and the prognosis was bad. Less than two months later after hearing the news, Patton was summoned back to California. His father had worsened and was going to have emergency surgery. Patton was there, and watched as they wheeled his father down the hall and into the operating room. The wait was interminable. Finally word came out to the waiting room that the elder Patton had made it through surgery and was resting quietly. By morning, his condition had stabilized. For three weeks the son put off returning to Hawaii, but by the middle of March could do so no longer. "I hated to leave before you were completely well," he wrote his father from the ship bound for Hawaii. "Now please as a favor to all of us...get well and strong so that you can enjoy life and we can enjoy having you."

It could not be that easy, though. Early in June, George Patton, Sr. died. There were no ships scheduled to leave Hawaii for several days and Patton was beside himself with grief. He knew he should have stayed longer. He knew he should not have spent so much of his life away from home. He could have done so much more for his father, he thought. By the time he reached California, after what must have been a dreadfully sad voyage, he had missed the funeral. He put on his dress uniform and went to the cemetery. He knew, he said, that "the grave no more held Papa than [did] one of his discarded suits hanging in a closet." While at the gravesite, Patton had a vision of his father, and then, a few days later, had a second vision of his father standing in the doorway of his study. Despite his tears, the vision was as clear as if he were alive. It gave him strength. "God grant that you see and appreciate my very piteous attempt to show here your lovely life," Patton wrote in memorial. "I never did much for you and you did all for me." Among all the letters of consolation that poured in, there was a touching note from John J. Pershing. "I know the high esteem in which you yourself held him," he wrote to his grieving young friend and fellow officer, "and knew him well enough to understand fully the reasons for your great admiration and affection." These words from Pershing meant a great deal to George S. Patton, Jr.

Like many officers during peacetime, Patton was shuttled about from post to post. From the spring of 1928 through the spring of 1935, Patton was back on the east coast, serving in the office of the chief of cavalry. His former riding partner Henry Stimson became the secretary of state under the new president, Herbert Hoover, and the two men revived their friendship. Patton was also reunited with Dwight Eisenhower who was transferred to the war department right around this same time. All was not happiness, even though they were glad to be back in Washington. In October 1929, Patton's mother died, followed within two years by his Aunt Nannie. He wrote a tender memorial to his mother in which he painfully admitted "I never really showed you in life the love I really felt nor my admiration for your courage and sporting acceptance of illness and losses. Children are cruel things."

Unfortunately, Patton could be cruel as an adult, too. He was getting older and, it appeared at times, embittered by his career. After a particularly bad fall in a polo match in which he sustained a concussion, he no longer seemed to hold his alcohol as well as he once did. He often drank too much and his temper was shorter than ever. He sometimes said hurtful things to Beatrice and his daughters when he was drinking and on occasion created embarrassing scenes in public when he would begin to recite poetry at inappropriate times.

If the officers in the American Army felt at loose ends during the 1920s and 1930s, the enlisted men truly suffered. Especially after the onset of the Great Depression soldiers found themselves grossly underpaid. For the veterans of the war who had been discharged at the end of the fighting, the government had planned to compensate their service by paying a bonus via bonds that would mature in 1945. As the economy toppled, however, many wanted and needed to cash in on that promise early. Some unemployed veterans had begun to show up at posts like Fort Myer, hoping to find a place to stay or at least a meal. Before long, tens of thousands had descended on the nation's capital hoping to goad Congress into taking some kind of action. It was a disgraceful symbol of how the country was neglecting its army and its soldiers. As thousands camped out around the city and showed up on the steps of the Capitol building to protest their plight, rumors swirled that there were revolutionary agitators in the midst of the genuine veterans hoping to foment trouble.

Already pressed from every imaginable direction for the economic crisis, President Hoover ordered that the protestors be removed from the streets of Washington. Army Chief of Staff Douglas MacArthur led the operation and, in fact, zealously exceeded his orders not to pursue the crowd should it retreat over the Anacostia River. As executive officer of the Third Cavalry Regiment, called out for this distasteful duty, Patton was not in overall command, but was at the center of what quickly evolved into a violent melee between horsemen, a detachment of bayonet-wielding infantry, and thousands of shocked protestors. The "Bonus March" as it was known, thereby came to a violent end, with Patton playing a prominent role, and immediately became a public relations disaster for the Hoover administration. It was a singularly shameful episode in how the government treated many of its discharged veterans during the tough years of the Great Depression. One of the marchers, in fact, was Joseph Angelo, the man who had pulled Patton into a foxhole after he had been shot back on the fields of France. Angelo had walked all the way from New Jersey to take part in the protest. "Major Ousts Vet Who Saved Life," one newspaper headline read, reporting that Patton and Angelo had had an unpleasant reunion. "Bonus Seeker Flees before Officer He Rescued on Battlefield." Patton, who was unapologetic about the way the marchers had been treated, fully believed that revolutionaries had infiltrated their ranks and caused the bulk of the troubles.

Outside of this episode, Patton's life was becoming more and more mundane and less and less how he imagined and hoped a career as an army officer would be. In 1934, oldest daughter Beatrice married army Lieutenant John Waters in the same church where George and Beatrice were married back in 1910. The ceremony was grand—almost an exact copy, in fact, of the previous Patton wedding. Outwardly, George Patton was the gracious father of the bride, smiling, chatting with visitors, and making toasts. Inside he felt every one of his 49 years and constantly feared that he was never going to get a true chance to distinguish himself on the battlefield. The army had become a tedious job. Memories of combat made day-to-day drudgery seem even more meaningless. He grew glumly convinced that he could look forward to no real future. On top of everything else, he suffered from the typical mental affliction known as the male midlife crisis. Irritated by his often erratic and usually sullen behavior, Beatrice bought him a book entitled *Change of Life in Men*. It infuriated him.

Over the course of these several years, Patton spent a year at the Army War College, the highest institution of professional education in the armed forces. At one point he traveled out to Kansas and dropped in on Fort Riley and Fort Leavenworth to watch maneuvers and catch up with some old friends. He even served another stint out in Hawaii and in 1938 was promoted to colonel and given command of the Fifth Cavalry Regiment at Fort Clark, just west of San Antonio, Texas. By the end of the decade he was back at Fort Myer, across the Potomac from the capital. Nothing seemed to be changing. Nothing he did satisfied his burning desire for action, distinction, and honor. Nothing seemed productive. It all began to seem meaningless.

The real importance of these difficult years was not in where he was posted or the different jobs he did, but the fact that he somehow, despite his dejection, never stopped writing, studying, and thinking about how a genuine soldier and warrior did his job in leading men into battle. He also wrote and thought constantly about tanks and how they should be used. Being back in the cavalry helped focus his mind back on the distinctive job cavalry served in combat and onto this he began to graft the experience he had gained through his exposure to tanks and mechanized warfare from World War I.

The memories of World War I, however, were beginning to be replaced by worries that another war was coming closer. In 1937, full-scale war broke out when Japan invaded China, continuing on a course that would soon make Japan the pre-eminent power in the Pacific region. Patton was in Hawaii until June 1937, and paid close attention to events from East Asia. Earlier that year, he wrote a report he titled "Surprise" about a Japanese sneak attack on Hawaii. He warned that "complete surprise offers the greatest opportunity for the successful capture of these islands." Some of Japan's island possessions were separated from the Hawaiian Islands by nothing more than "the loneliest sea lanes in the world," and who was to say that there were not already Japanese divisions on those islands training for an invasion. It was all a distinct possibility, including the use of carrier-based aircraft and submarines. He admitted, however, that this was unlikely. Few took such a notion seriously.

The rest of the world was in turmoil as well as East Asia. Italy had invaded Ethiopia and the League of Nations, created at the end of the World War to preserve the peace and avoid any more wars, had protested but done nothing of substance. In Germany, Adolph Hitler was in power and was openly rearming the German military, while the League and the international community did nothing. In September 1938, eager to avoid war, Britain and France agreed to let Germany take a region of Czechoslovakia known as the Sudetenland with the promise that Hitler would make no aggressive moves in return. Patton was disgusted. Six months later the German army marched into the rest of Czechoslovakia and six months after that, invaded Poland. World War II, the war that would make Patton a legend, had begun.

Chapter 8

INTO THE FIGHT AT LAST

Where are they now, the horses who fought for us in France,
The horses of the limber and the gun?
They shared our toil and triumph and they shared our joy and pain,
But we left them, yes, we left them every one.

In September 1939, the same month Germany invaded Poland, the U.S. Army received a new chief of staff. George C. Marshall would prove to be one of the most important figures in the war and was instrumental in transforming the army of the 1920s and 1930s into a viable fighting force. He especially wanted to usher some of the older officers, men who had spent the two decades since the last war shuffling from post to post and losing their fighting spirit, into retirement. He wanted to clear the war for young and energetic officers who would be able to lead the United States Army into the next war. Patton was worried. Even though both men were stationed at Fort Myer, and even though Marshall actually lived with Patton for a while as his own quarters were being refurbished, Patton feared he would be one of those older men sent out to pasture. Younger officers were being promoted and moved around as Europe again exploded into war. Patton remained at Fort Myer and heard nothing about him being reassigned to a more active position.

Marshall, however, had no intention of shuffling Patton off the main stage. In fact, he believed Patton was perfect for the rebuilt army. He was "by far the best tank man in the Army," said Marshall. "I know this from the First World War. I watched him closely when he commanded the first tanks we ever had." Marshall was well aware that Patton was a difficult man sometimes, but he thought he knew how to handle him. Patton's drive, energy, and thoroughness were all far too valuable to let go to waste.

Marshall also knew that the future of the army lay in tanks and armored forces, not in the horse cavalry. Patton, of course, needed no convincing of this, having been moving in this direction since the end of the last war. In case he needed a reminder, though, in the spring of 1940 he served as an umpire for the U.S. Third Army's maneuver exercises in Louisiana. There, a division of horse cavalry was soundly beaten by tank and motorized forces organized into what was labeled an "armored division." While the exercise was going on, Germany invaded France and Belgium. The slashing speed of the attack, spearheaded with tanks, showed the world in graphic detail the same lessons that Patton was learning in Louisiana.

In truth, Patton had been rather disappointed in just how poorly the horse cavalry had faired in the maneuvers when pitted against tanks and trucks. His long-held feelings and affinity for horses, however, did not keep him from acting on what was now obvious to almost anyone with good sense: the horse was no longer going to have a decisive role on the battlefields of the future. While some of his closest companions in the cavalry remained loyal to the horse and disparaged the effect that technology would have on the battlefield, Patton fully embraced the new realities of combat. Over the previous years he had read with great interest articles on tanks and their use by German military thinkers. Now seeing the obvious put on graphic display in both Louisiana and northern France made up his mind.

Even though he had spent most of his professional life in the cavalry, Patton had learned its lessons without becoming unbreakably bound to the vehicle. Horses were simply the *vehicle* cavalries used to achieve their purposes. Or, to put it a different way, cavalry was a job and horses were what had traditionally carried out that job. Now, the horse had simply been replaced by a motorized vehicle. The job, really, did not change that much. In one of the last articles he wrote that evoked the memory of the horse cavalry, he said that the "secret of success in mounted operations is to GRAB THE ENEMY BY THE NOSE AND KICK HIM IN THE PANTS." As always—as it had been since the days of Alexander the Great or of Napoleon's dashing corps commander Murat—the kick in the pants would be generously applied by the cavalry. It was the only force that could get quickly around to where the kick would be applied. The only difference now was that instead of horses delivering the kick, it would be tanks.

The decisions of a handful of people now came together to rescue George S. Patton from staff duty on the tranquil hillside across the Potomac from the ever more bustling capital. George Marshall had long since determined that Patton was too good and too energetic a soldier to be shown the door. Early in July, Patton's old friend and riding buddy Henry Stimson became President Franklin Roosevelt's secretary of war. A short letter of congratulations served to remind Stimson that Patton was still close at hand, ready and eager to spring into action. Finally, in the summer of 1940, Patton learned that his friend Adna Chaffee would be taking command of the army's first armored corps, made up of the First and Second Armored Divisions. He quickly wrote his friend another letter of congratulations, again not asking for anything special, but no doubt hoping that the letter would keep Patton's name at the front of his friend's memory. Chaffee responded in a way that no doubt gave Patton a boost of much-needed encouragement: "I hope things will work out favorably for you. I shall always be happy to know that you are around close in any capacity when there is fighting to be done."

In the middle of July, Patton was taking a short leave up in Massachusetts, visiting Beatrice, who was spending a good bit of her time there. On the morning of the 15th, as he perused the newspapers, he saw a story about himself. He discovered he had been given command of one of the armored brigades of the Second Armored Division, based at Fort Benning, Georgia. He was ecstatic. He fired off letters to Chaffee, Marshall, and Charles L. Scott, commander of the Second Armored Division, thanking them for giving him the chance for a tank command. "I am sure that this most happy detail was due to your efforts," he told Chaffee, "and I appreciate it very much." Marshall thought the assignment would be "just the sort of thing you would like to do at the moment. Also," he added, "I felt that no one could do that particular job better."

Patton left for Georgia almost immediately and, less than two weeks after reading about his new assignment in the papers, took command of his brigade. When filled out to full strength, Patton would be in command of 350 officers, 5,550 men, 383 tanks, 202 armored cars, and two dozen pieces of artillery. "Army Horseman to Lead Ft. Benning Tank Brigade," read the headline in the newspaper.

By the end of July, however, there were only 99 officers and 2,220 men in the entire division, less than half of what was supposed to fill out Patton's brigade. There was hardly any equipment, and the training grounds, repair shops, and barracks all had to be built from the ground up. Most of all of the tanks were of World War I vintage and hopelessly out of date. They could be used for training purposes, though, until more modern tanks began to come out of American factories. It was the tank-training center at Bourg, France in 1918 all over again. But again, Patton jumped into the job with abandon. He gave an introductory speech to the soldiers as they arrived, now coming in at the rate of about 100 per day. He knew that the facilities and the brigade did not look like much to the incoming soldiers, but he knew that things would be changing very soon. And once that happened, he told his men, "may God have mercy on our enemies; they will need it."

When Patton heard that his old friend and fellow tank-booster Dwight Eisenhower was back in the United States after a posting overseas in the Philippines, he wrote and suggested that Ike request a transfer to the armored corps. "It would be great to be in the tanks once more, and even better to be associated with you again," Ike replied to his old friend. Patton said that he would be happy to have Eisenhower as his chief of staff or maybe even a regimental commander in his brigade. As things worked out, Eisenhower was transferred elsewhere. They would come in contact again, however, in the future.

Meanwhile, Patton continued to train his men relentlessly. He was everywhere at once, inspecting, ordering, cajoling, bellowing, cursing, and insisting on perfection in any- and everything. All fell under his unblinking gaze. He demanded that his men have clean uniforms and shined shoes. He would stop his jeep and loudly berate a soldier for an insufficient salute. He knew it all seemed cruel, but there was a reason behind his apparent fanaticism. "If you can't get them to salute when they should salute," he explained to his friend Harry Semmes, "how are you going to get them to die for their country?"

In public speeches to local citizens' groups, he compared his tankers to the cavalry of Civil War Generals Ulysses S. Grant and J.E.B. Stuart, along with that of Napoleon. In training, his main concern was to instill in his men an unbreakable fighting spirit that could carry the day against any opposition. He cultivated what he called a desperate determination to always move forward and to not be stopped by any obstacle. "If I can get this across," he confided, "we will be very hard to beat." The spirits of his men also counted for much. To boost morale and the image of armored forces in the eyes of the country, he organized a 400 mile road trip down to Panama City, Florida, and back. People all along the route gazed in wonder as 1,100 vehicles creaked and squeaked along the roads of Georgia, Florida, and a corner of Alabama. It was a fascinating spectacle.

The exercise was good publicity for both the tanks and George S. Patton, personally. "Gen. Patton of the Cavalry Sets Fast Pace for the Tank Corps—Army Knows His Name as Synonym for Daring Action," hailed an article in the Washington Sunday paper. Patton was a "hard-riding, hard-hitting 'fightin' man' of the old school," it said. Other reporters boasted that Patton could get a tank that was hopelessly mired in a creek unstuck and back on the bank "practically by the power of his curses" alone. Patton, everyone could agree, was certainly a colorful leader. He appeared on the cover of *Life* magazine, standing up in the turret of a tank, scowling menacingly at who-knew-what out in the distance. As he had in the First World War, Patton wanted his men to look and feel distinctive. Now instead of just a patch, he designed an entire new uniform for his tank soldiers. It consisted of a dark green jacket with bright buttons down each side, dark green pants loaded with extra pockets and padding, and a hat that looked remarkably like a football helmet. He himself modeled it for the newspaper photographers, and subsequently readers all over the country got a good look at it. Reactions were mixed, but most people thought it looked ridiculous, which it really did. His men kept their standard uniforms for now.

As Adna Chaffee's health began to decline, General Scott was transferred from division command in Georgia to Fort Knox, Kentucky, to take temporary command of the whole armored corps. When Scott left, Patton moved up to take his place as acting commander of the Second Armored Division. He was soon promoted to major general and given permanent command. Beatrice came down to Georgia to be with her husband and they moved into the commander's house on the post. By the spring of 1941, the entire division had over 11,000 men and 2,000 vehicles and Patton was in charge of it all. When the division drove up to Tennessee in June for maneuvers, it again brought out thousands of spectators. Traveling in two columns, the division took up 60 miles of road. A few months later the Second Armored Division headed down to Louisiana to take part in an even larger exercise in which 27 full divisions took part. In November, there was still another exercise, this one in the Carolinas. In each, Patton's units were distinctive for their bold action and Patton himself learned more about how to command tanks in action.

A few days after Patton and his division returned to Fort Benning from the Carolina maneuvers, Japan attacked Pearl Harbor and the United States was drawn into the Second World War. He gathered his soldiers together for a talk. "Probably the next time we face opponents," Patton told the men of his division, "they will not be friendly enemies but malignant foes. Next time you will be opposed not by white flags but by hot lead." It was one of the last speeches he would make to the division as its commander, because Patton was moving up. Shortly before the country entered the war, General Scott was transferred to the Middle East to be the senior American military observer with the British forces operating there. In January, Patton was given command of the First Armored Corps.

Dwight Eisenhower was also moving up the ladder, although he was staying in Washington. Ike had been promoted to chief of the operations division that worked very closely with Chief of Staff George Marshall to plan the specific when, where, and how of whatever attacks the fighting forces would then carry out. Patton carefully watched the career of his friend and believed that such a position suited Eisenhower well. "You name them; I'll shoot them," he wrote Ike in February. Patton soon received a clue just as to where the operations planners were envisioning as the first opportunity for American tanks to take on the enemy. He was ordered to California to scout out, create, and command a training center specifically designed for the rigors of desert fighting, one that could closely replicate conditions in North Africa.

Patton ran the desert training center as he had done all his other commands. There was the strictest discipline, the most orderly and well-groomed soldiers, and the toughest work from dawn until dusk, every day. He had each soldier running a mile in 10 minutes with a rifle and full field pack. As always he seemed to be everywhere at once and rarely did a day go by without almost every soldier in the corps seeing him at one time or another, seemingly just when something had gone wrong. When he discovered trouble, there was always a barrage of profanity before he rolled up his own sleeves and helped get to the bottom of whatever the problem happened to be. He always wore his toughest facial expression—the one he had spent years cultivating before the mirror—and threatened to shoot anyone who was photographed smiling. As the training went on, with 13 major exercises in the first three weeks, he could soon report that his men were doing better each day and that they were getting "up to the level of the Roman legions."

From time to time, Patton also typically worried that his remote location across the continent from Washington would result in his being forgotten when the time came to assign units and commanders to active duty. He penned letter after letter to his superiors, constantly reminding them that he was still hard at work and ready to go at a moment's notice. In one he requested that when the serious fighting started, he be given a chance "to prove in blood what I have learned in sweat." As it turned out, his superiors had no inclination to forget about the eager tank commander out in the deserts of California. High command was seriously contemplating the use of an armored corps in action soon and Patton had long since been selected to command it.

Since the entry of the United States into the war, American and British planners had been trying to determine where and when American soldiers would first see action. Though Marshall had recently dispatched Dwight Eisenhower to London as his special representative to Prime Minister Winston Churchill, the two nations' planning staffs were having trouble determining the best course of action for the new ally. Meanwhile, the Soviet Union, having been invaded by the German army in the summer of 1941, and now bearing the brunt of Hitler's forces alone, clamored endlessly for the British and Americans to open up a second front immediately, if not sooner, to take some of the pressure off the Soviet army. Marshall was adamant that any offensive against Germany be a major operation and not simply nip at the edges, especially the southern edges, of Europe. Realistically, however, there was little hope that a major invasion of northern Europe could be mounted in the immediate future.

On the southern shore of the Mediterranean, in North Africa, German tanks and troops under General Erwin Rommel were driving British forces eastward toward Egypt and the Suez Canal at a rate that alarmed officials in London. While Churchill was in Washington in the summer of 1942, word reached him that the stronghold of Tobruk had fallen to Rommel and the British forces were falling back into Egypt. President Roosevelt made it clear that the United States was ready to do anything Churchill wanted in order to stop the Germans' eastward march. Marshall suggested a complete armored division and Churchill gladly accepted. Soon Marshall was on the telephone calling for Patton to come to Washington.

As it became obvious to American planners that doing nothing until they could orchestrate the major invasion of Europe was not an option, they began to formulate interim plans. The great fear was that the Russian army might well disintegrate at the hands of the Germans if another front could not distract some of Hitler's tanks. The situation in North Africa seemed especially appropriate for quick American action, given that one of the army's foremost tank commanders had been working for just such an operation in the deserts of California. Churchill himself was pressing for it. American troops seemed ready for it. Roosevelt and Marshall finally agreed.

The operation was code-named TORCH, and it was to consist of combined U.S. and British landings across the beach in far western North Africa. George Patton would be in command of the "Western Task Force," that would sail across the Atlantic from the United States, land on the western coast of Morocco and secure the region for the Allies. Since Morocco was controlled by the French and since the fall of their nation in the summer of 1940, the French were officially allies of Hitler. No one knew for certain what the reaction would be to American soldiers storming across the Moroccan beaches. Patton was ready for anything. The operation was set to go sometime that fall, most likely October or November. Early in August, Patton boarded an airplane and headed for England to take part in the detailed planning for TORCH.

Once again Patton found himself in wartime London. Instead of staying at the Tower of London as he had done in 1918, he now bunked at a fine hotel. There was a warm reunion with Eisenhower and the two quickly got down to work. Some evenings after the official work was done, the two friends stayed up until long past midnight talking about the world situation and the war, and reminiscing over all the times that they had imagined taking part in something just like this. It seemed a lot like old times, but with one little difference. Patton felt that all the American officers he was running into—even Eisenhower himself—seemed extremely pro-British, and less like regular U.S. Army officers, he confided to his diary. While this caused him no great concern now, he did make a wary note of it. In the future, it would come to bother him more and more, especially when he thought he saw his friend Ike acting more like an ally than an American. For now, however, he kept such thoughts to himself.

In letters to Beatrice, Patton provided a running commentary on London at war. He could hardly buy anything, the rationing was so severe. "The coffee is artificial and one is always hungry." "The only thing they seem to have lots of is smoked salmon," he complained. Perhaps to reassure her he also explained that "all of us think that if there ever were any pretty women in England they must have died." In all, he was in England for about two weeks of planning and meetings. By the time he headed back to Washington, he was getting worried that most of the other planners were far too timid. "I feel that I am the only true gambler in the whole outfit." He also believed that Eisenhower was getting megalomania. Eisenhower, for his part, was thrilled to have Patton leading part of the operation.

The date of the landings was set for November 8. Patton's force would be sailing straight to Africa from Norfolk, Virginia, with no stopover en route. He and his troops would be coming ashore somewhere in the vicinity of Casablanca. Beyond these few operational certainties, however, there was only guesswork. The navy was worried about the possibility of high crashing surf along the coastline. No one still seemed to know for sure exactly what the French reaction would be. Patton maintained an unshakable faith that the operation would be a success no matter how much fighting would be necessary. And he was ready to lead men into the fight. "The more I dig into this thing," he wrote to his old comrade from the Second Armored Division, Charles Scott, "the more I am sure that the only thing that will win it will be leadership, speed, and drive, plus sound tactics." All were Patton's strengths, and he knew it. "When I think of the greatness of my job and realize that I am what I am, I am amazed, but on reflection, who is as good as I am? I know of no one." As for the soldiers he would be commanding, they were "the best trained troops of all arms this country can produce," he said.

As the date of departure drew near, Patton grew more excited. There was plenty to do to keep him occupied. He found time to write numerous letters; several were of the "if you are reading this I've been killed on the battlefield" variety. He stopped by one last time to visit with George Marshall, and then went to Walter Reed Army Hospital to see the ailing John J. Pershing. Patton told his old boss that he was taking the same pistol to Europe that he had carried on the expedition into Mexico. "I hope you kill some Germans with it," Pershing said. As Patton left, Pershing took his hand and gave it a strong squeeze. "Goodbye George," he said. "God bless and keep you and give you victory." Patton responded with the crispest salute he could muster. As Pershing returned it, the years seemed to drop away and he was the same vigorous leader who had taken Patton to Mexico with him. His eyes heavy with emotion, Patton turned and left. He would never see Pershing again, yet the older Pershing would ultimately outlive George Patton by three years.

Shortly before he left for Africa Patton, along with Admiral H. Kent Hewitt, who would be in command of the ships carrying Patton's task force, called on President Roosevelt at the White House. Patton assured the president that both he and Hewitt fully understood just how important this operation was. It would be the first time American troops went into battle in the European theater and a good showing was absolutely crucial. Over in the Pacific, Japanese expansion had finally been checked at the Battle of the Coral Sea and at Midway, and the marines were trying to secure the island of Guadalcanal. Not much in the way of concrete advances were happening against Germany though, and that needed to change quickly, or the whole "Europe First" strategy that the American and British had agreed on might be in jeopardy, not to mention the continued ability of the Soviet army to stand up to the Germans. Patton was not too impressed with what he saw of Roosevelt's grasp of military matters. Roosevelt, on the other hand, described Patton as a joy.

Bea flew with him down to Norfolk for his departure. As they approached the airfield for landing, peering out of the little windows of the plane, they could see below them all the ships of the task force riding calmly at anchor in the numerous slips at the naval base. After the plane touched down, they said their good-byes. Somehow Bea kept from crying. Patton slipped her a last note as he headed off. "It will probably be some time before you get a letter from me," it read, "but I will be thinking of you and loving you."

For the trip across the Atlantic, Patton would have the captain's cabin on board the flotilla's flagship, the cruiser *Augusta*. He spent the last night before departure on the ship. "God grant that I do my full duty to my men and myself," he wrote in his diary before shutting his eyes. Shortly after 8:00 the next morning, the *Augusta* led the task force out to sea. Patton was impressed by the smoothness and orderly nature of the operation. The ships passed through the belts of minefields that surrounded the Norfolk naval base and protected the entrances to the Chesapeake Bay. All together there were about 100 ships in the convoy.

The crossing was to take about two weeks. Since he was headed for an Islamic country, Patton read the Koran while at sea. Every night all the ships' navigation lights were doused for fear of German submarines, but Patton had a light in his cabin for reading. He exercised whenever he got a chance, because the food was superior and he worried he would get fat. One night about a week into the voyage, a strong north wind kicked up and the seas got rough. The tossing and heaving made sleep almost impossible and then word came that there were German subs all through the area. It was a bad night. So bad, he said the next morning, things were bound to get better now. He was wrong. The following night was even worse as the winds kicked up to 40 miles an hour. Who knew how the seas would be when it came time to go ashore? "I have done some extra praying," Patton wrote in his diary.

As the day approached, still no one was entirely sure how the French would react. Would they fight? If so, tenaciously? Would it be a drawn out battle? Or would they immediately come over to the allied side? Eisenhower had set up temporary headquarters at Gibraltar and there were rumors of top secret contacts with the French forces. Then, just as credible, came rumors that the French were indeed going to put up a fight. The uncertainty made for a difficult wait. "Every once in a while the tremendous responsibility of this job lands on me like a ton of bricks," he wrote. In the midst of the waiting, Patton issued an address to all his men. It was all of his ideas of war distilled down into a last energetic and exhorting pep talk. "When the great day of battle comes, remember your training, and remember above all that speed and vigor of attack are the sure roads to success and you must succeed—for to retreat is as cowardly as it is fatal. Indeed, once landed, retreat is impossible. Americans do not surrender." They could not rest even for a moment. "A pint of sweat will save a gallon of blood." On November 7, the convoy parted into three sections that would hit three different Moroccan beaches. That night at 10:30 he went to bed dressed for action.

He awoke with a start at 2:00 in the morning on November 8. The ship had stopped moving. He pulled on his boots and went topside. The sea was smooth as glass. He could see the lights of Casablanca burning brightly on shore. Just up the dark coastline off to the northeast, he could also see the lights of the town of Fedala. That was where his men would hit the beach. Off in the darkness somewhere on the glassy sea, there were other destroyers being led in close to the shore by a submarine. For a few more hours there was silence except for the lapping of the ocean along the sides of the *Augusta*. The transport ships made ready to unload. The sky in the east began to lighten. Suddenly, the big guns on shore erupted. Shells began crashing into the sea, sending geysers of water spraying into the air. The fleets' guns, including those of the *Augusta* roared back. George Patton was at last seeing action in the largest war of the twentieth century.

The southern wing of Patton's task force accomplished its mission quickly, capturing the town of Safi and some troops of the famous French Foreign Legion. Where Patton was though, things were not going as smoothly. At some point in the morning, enemy bombers appeared in the skies heading for the troop transports. Amazingly, they were driven off by several ships' guns without any serious damage. *Augusta* and the other destroyers kept up a constant barrage against on-shore targets. Everyone on board, Patton included, had to stuff his ears with cotton to stand the racket. (Days later, from the comfort of the Shell Oil Company building that Patton and his staff had taken over as a headquarters, he would write that naval battles were not all that impressive because they were too impersonal.) Several French ships tried to get out of the harbor but were pounded so relentlessly by the American destroyers they had to turn back. Patton and his aides and orderlies did not get ashore until almost 1:30 in the afternoon. There was still sporadic gunfire along the beaches, but none of it threatened Patton or his men. All along the coastline thousands of American soldiers splashed onto the beaches and fought their way into the towns of Morocco. By evening, there was no sign that the French were going to surrender, but at the same time, they were not putting up much of a determined fight. Patton spent the night at a hotel that had had its electricity knocked out by the shelling.

The next morning before dawn, Patton was out on the beaches and out in the water over his belt, helping more of the troops unload. Barking orders and cursing constantly, he pulled boats onto the sand, spurred his men to action, and berated anyone not doing his duty. He came across a soldier curled up on the sand, muttering incoherently in fear. Patton kicked him hard in the behind and he jumped right up and went to work. More and more troops and equipment came ashore all day long and soon Casablanca was surrounded.

By nightfall on November 10, the French commander in town sent word of his willingness to surrender and order a stop to all the fighting throughout French North Africa. The next morning, Patton and the French commanders met at the Hotel Miramar in Fedala to end the fighting. Unexpectedly, Patton demanded a promise from his opponents, a promise he expected them to keep as honorable officers of the French army. If they would give him their "word of honor that there will be no further firing on American troops and ships, you may retain your arms and carry on as before—but under my orders," he added. Patton clearly realized that his relatively small forces was by no means sufficient to be an army of occupation and, frankly, took a great chance in doing this that one or several of the French officers would not go back on their word. But they did not. Patton wheeled out carts of champagne and proposed a toast "to the resumption of the age-old friendship between France and America." His knowledge of France, his ability to speak French, and the insight he had gained into the French military mind while studying at their academies in his lengthy travels throughout that country, had served him well. It turned out to be a happy fifty-seventh birthday for George Patton.

It had not been a bloodless battle. Among the American troops there were 337 killed, 637 wounded, 122 missing and 71 captured. Patton attended memorial services for the American soldiers who had been killed and then for the French soldiers who had lost their lives.

Over the next few days, Patton traveled a great deal and met with numerous dignitaries and leaders. He proved that he was a capable diplomat as well as soldier. First up though, was a quick flight to Gibraltar to brief Eisenhower in person on the Moroccan operation. Patton did not like what he found as he recounted the events to his old friend. Ike had taken to calling gasoline "petrol" as the British did. Other British words peppered his conversation. Patton worried about what this might mean for American soldiers if Eisenhower, who had been designated as commander in chief of all American forces in the European Theater of Operations, was thinking less like an American commander and more like an allied commander. It could not be good news. "I truly fear that London had conquered Abilene," he wrote to Beatrice, referring to the little Kansas town where Eisenhower had grown up. Petrol was only the beginning. The trend would, in fact, continue to the point at which Patton grew to think that Eisenhower was not thinking like an American soldier anymore. He was an ally now, instead. It annoyed Patton, but Patton never seemed to grasp, or at least he never admitted, the tremendous diplomatic job Eisenhower was trying to accomplish. He did later acknowledge that he must have lacked "something which makes the politicians trust Ike." Patton the soldier would spend the war being a soldier. Eisenhower the soldier would spend the war being a diplomat, not because he wanted to, but because it was his job. Sometimes the tasks seemed, at least to men like Patton, incompatible.

For his part, Patton often tried Eisenhower's patience. It surprised no one who knew him that Patton had a tendency to speak first—and usually with profane and boisterous energy—and think only afterward. Ike encouraged him to think before he spoke, and to be "less flip in my conversation on military matters." Eisenhower was particularly concerned that American generals not speak out against the English generals, their fighting styles or quality, or speak derisively about the status of the alliance. He vowed that if Patton "or anyone else criticizes the British, by God I will reduce him to his permanent grade and send him home." Clearly Ike was sensitive about the job he had to do, and was sensitive to British feelings. Quite probably he also realized that such sensitivity would inevitably raise questions about him being an ally first or an American first, as Patton had already privately wondered. No matter. The success of the war effort depended on a solid alliance and no one on his watch, under his command, was going to jeopardize that by speech or by action.

Despite their different positions and responsibilities, Eisenhower and Patton remained friends. They often seemed to need each other a great deal. It would not be long, however, before their friendship would be sorely tested. Soon the soldier would be causing troubles for the diplomat even more than the diplomat was now beginning to irritate the soldier.

As Patton's plane carried him back across the Strait of Gibraltar to Morocco, thousands of miles to the east the extent of a recent British victory was becoming clear. General Bernard Montgomery, "Monty" to his men, had decisively defeated Rommel at a place called El Alamein in Egypt, and now Rommel's army was in headlong retreat westward toward its bases in Tunisia. Egypt was saved from the Germans. Hard on Rommel's heels were Monty and the British army, determined not to let up the chase. An American force was quickly assembled to press eastward toward Tunisia in hopes of catching the Germans in a vise with the British coming from the east. Patton, however, would be remaining in Morocco.

November passed into December and Patton grew restless and bored. Once again he longed to be where the action was, but had personally seen none at all for over a month. He was certainly comfortable and treated well. "The Arab idea of hospitality is profusion," he said, adding, "Mama must have been part Arab." Being overwhelmed by welcome and acting almost as a Roman proconsul in a far-off province may have suited other men, but not George Patton. Not for long, at least. In letters to Beatrice he continued to grouse about Eisenhower and worry about being forgotten. He was getting to know the Sultan of Morocco pretty well, and he was keeping in touch with what was going on at the far-off front, but it wasn't enough. From Beatrice came letters telling of her taking tea at the White House with Eleanor Roosevelt and going with Mamie Eisenhower to meet women who were sending collections of canning supplies to England. She did her best to encourage her husband to hang in there. "I feel sure that you are marked by destiny," she told him, and "I am willing to wait on God for that." Patton believed it, too. He was just having a little more trouble waiting on God.

Chapter 9

RISKING LIFE AND CAREER

Pale was her face with anguish
Wet were her eyes with tears,
As she gazed at the twisted corpses
Cut off in their earliest years.

Off to the east in the deserts of Tunisia, the noose was tightening around the neck of Rommel's army. Nevertheless, the German general and his army continued to fight tenaciously. Early in 1943, he saw a chance to hit the American forces that were coming in from the west with a force strong enough so that, if things went right, the Americans would be forced to retreat. Rommel would then be able to keep his communication lines open back to the coastal cities of Tunis and Bizerte, could hold open an escape route back to the coast should one become necessary, and prevent his force from being surrounded. He set his sights on the American Second Corps and quickly began drawing up a plan.

The American troops of the Second Corps were inexperienced, overextended and, frankly, poorly led. The Second Corps commander was Lloyd Fredendall, who, more than anyone else was causing Eisenhower the most grief by his inappropriate anti-British comments. Beyond that, he was out of touch with his men and was always quarreling with his subordinates. He openly disliked General Orlando Ward, the commander of his First Armored Division. When Eisenhower had mentioned Fredendall to one of his British colleagues, the response was "I'm sure you must have better men than that."

One day early in March, Patton was out riding a horse, yet another welcome accommodation by his North African hosts. Upon returning to his headquarters, he found an urgent message from Eisenhower. Fredendall's command had been demolished by Rommel's attack at a place in the Tunisian mountains called Kasserine Pass. The soldiers had been thrown back in chaos, American supply depots were threatened, and Fredendall had been summarily dismissed by an angry and frustrated Eisenhower. Newspapers in the United States and Britain were running stories that made it look like the Americans could not fight. Morale had been crippled. Ike was now offering command of the 80,000-plus men of the Second Corps, and the rebuilding job that would come with it, to Patton. Knowing well his friend's impetuous nature, Ike warned Patton he wanted him "as a corps commander—not a casualty."

When Patton arrived at Second Corps headquarters, he was stunned by the disarray. His first morning there, he went to the mess hall to have breakfast at 7:00 and found no one there but another officer eating by himself. He was outraged. He ordered that the mess hall be closed every morning at 7:30 and if anyone arrived later, he would not get breakfast. Discipline, dress, soldierly deportment, everything was terrible. Hardly anyone saluted and those who did, did so sloppily. Little wonder the battle had gone so terribly wrong, thought Patton. If the men did not act like soldiers, how could they be expected to fight like soldiers? He would fix that, but he would have to do so quickly, for Second Corps was already scheduled to take part in an important diversionary offensive to coincide with a major attack on the German lines by the British army.

"Each time a soldier knotted his necktie, threaded his leggings, and buckled on his heavy steel helmet, he was forcibly reminded that Patton had come to command the II Corps," wrote General Omar Bradley. When Patton arrived in Tunisia, he met up for the first time with Bradley, whom Ike had dispatched to the area several days earlier to be his personal representative. Patton instead quickly arranged for Bradley to be his deputy commander. The two had never served together before, and, quite honestly, did not have much in common in the way of style, personality, or background. Bradley could not abide the torrents of profanity Patton was liable to unleash at a moment's notice, and believed that Patton talked down to his soldiers. His Jekyll and Hyde persona annoyed and puzzled Bradley.

Quite simply, George Patton often put on an act for his soldiers, usually to make a point of some sort about discipline, behavior, or training, and Omar Bradley was never exactly sure which of Patton's angry outbursts was an act, and which profane tirades were genuine rage breaking the sur-

face. After one particularly violent reaction against his men for not having their bayonets fixed to their rifles while practicing a beach assault,
Patton leaned over to Bradley and remarked "chew them out and they'll
remember it." Hardly anyone could tell when Patton's rage was an act,
and that was precisely the way he wanted it. He wanted his soldiers to listen and remember his orders and this was the way he figured they were
most likely to do just that. Whether it was an act or poor self-control,
Bradley did not like it.

Patton later gave a clue as to why he was as tough as he was, and why
he demanded a standard of perfection that seemed to men like Bradley,
sometimes to border on the abuse of his authority. "Discipline can only be
obtained," he explained, "when all officers are so imbued with the sense of
their lawful obligation to their men and to their country that they cannot
tolerate negligence. Officers who fail to correct errors or praise excellence
are valueless in peace and dangerous misfits in war." Bradley was disgusted
though, at many of Patton's means of correcting errors. That Patton's
praise was often as effusive as his curses, and that behind his purposeful
lack of sentimentality he harbored genuine affection for his men was, perhaps, lost on Bradley most of the time. After all, the colorful outbursts and
outlandish behavior were what got the attention. Here was another way
in which the two men parted ways. Patton craved attention, even thrived
on it. Bradley was so low-key he became known to his men as "the G.I.
General." The famous American war correspondent and unabashed
Bradley fan, Ernie Pyle, christened him that. Never did Bradley flaunt his
rank. Patton always did. The relationship between the two men during
the war usually remained civil, but it was often strained. Behind Patton's
back, Bradley was sometimes bitterly critical of him.

As the new commander of the Second Corps, General Patton and his
men would be under British General Sir Harold Alexander, the commander of all the Allied forces in North Africa and a man Patton liked
very much—at least most of the time. Alexander stipulated that Patton's
corps would attack the flank of the German army and draw their attention, while British Commander Bernard Montgomery attacked toward
the town of Tunis. Patton was ready and understood the strategy, but was
just as determined to re-energize the fighting spirit of his men with a bold
victory and to prove that American troops were the equal of their British
allies. He also saw that the mission had at least the possibility of achieving an actual breakthrough, rather than simply providing the threat of a
breakthrough that Alexander's more conservative plan had in mind. At
any chance, he vowed that he would push his men as far forward as he
could.

The offensive began on the night of March 16 in weather that was cold and wet. On several days after the battle had begun, it was simply too wet to move, let alone attack. It did not seem like the desert fighting he had been training for in California. When weather permitted, he urged his men forward, appearing in person to exhort, demand, threaten, and encourage. "I feel terribly sorry for the men in this cold," he wrote Beatrice during a lull in the fighting. The men fought tenaciously. Several days into the fighting, Patton's men caught a German column in the open and attacked in a daylong battle. At the end, after losing over 30 tanks, the Germans pulled back in defeat. In celebration of their valor, Patton arranged for his men to have a steak dinner and a two-day period of rest. As the broad allied offensive continued, Alexander gradually approved more action for Patton's corps. The German position lines began to crumble all around.

Through all these days of combat, Patton made it a point to visit his wounded men in the field hospitals. To do so was tough for him sometimes, but he was determined to make himself seen among the wounded just as he had among the front line troops. Often they were the same young men. All, who were able, seemed eager and anxious for him to speak with them individually. He felt that the treatment of the wounded was much better than it had been in the last war, and he certainly would have known. Even the hospital food was better, he thought.

On April 1, Patton's personal aide Dick Jensen was killed by a bomb dropped from a German airplane. Patton had sent Jensen out with Bradley, a couple of other generals, and some other aides to a command post closer to the fighting. Patton was not with Jenson when he was killed and sadly believed that his aide's death was partly his fault. Like Patton, Jensen was from Southern California. In fact, his mother was one of Patton's old childhood friends. He had grown to think of Jensen like a son, and his death hit Patton hard. "I am really more broken up over Dick than I can express," he said to one of his fellow generals, Geoffrey Keyes. "I did not know how fond I was of him." They wrapped Jensen in a white mattress cover and buried him in a cemetery at the little Tunisian village of Gafsa. There were no coffins available because there was no wood. "I shall miss him very much," an emotional Patton wrote to Bea. To his diary, he confided that "I can't see the reason that such fine young men get killed."

Although Patton never could replace his almost paternal feelings for Dick Jensen, Jensen's job as Patton's primary aide would later be ably filled by a remote acquaintance from Beatrice's side of the family, army Lieutenant Charles Codman.

The Allies followed up the March attack with continued pressure on the Germans. Newspapers back in the United States wrote glowingly of the American progress in the offensive. Stinging memories from the disaster at Kasserine Pass began to be less bitter in the light of this new fighting success. Nevertheless, there were still problems. British commanders ordered Patton not to continue his attack toward the coastline, which Patton was distinctly in favor of doing. An attack of this nature would pinch the German forces in two, and those that did not surrender immediately could be beaten piecemeal. Typically, he was convinced beyond a doubt that the only reason he had been stopped was so that the British would be able to press the attack themselves and gain the triumph alone. The thought made him angrier the more he thought about it. He swallowed his temper, though, because "there was nothing else to do, but I can't see how Ike can let them pull his leg so. It is awful." Patton came to think he would rather go back to planning the next stage of the American offensive beyond North Africa than remain here in Tunisia and be humiliated and infuriated. But until different orders came down, he stayed where he was.

Gradually Patton was growing incensed by still another snub by the British. This one, however, had a much more immediate effect on his men. He was frustrated by the lack of support from the Allied air forces his men were receiving for their attacks. Dick Jensen's death from German aircraft only highlighted the nasty results when enemy planes could roam the skies at will. He did not hesitate to explain the matter directly to British Air Vice Marshal Arthur Coningham, a man every bit as opinionated and outspoken as Patton himself. There was bound to be friction. Coningham responded that perhaps the real problem was that the soldiers of the Second Corps were not tough enough. Such an accusation dredged up the memories of Kasserine that the American commanders, Patton included of course, would certainly rather forget. The two eventually had a heated face-to-face meeting about the problem that at one point deteriorated into a shouting match. When Eisenhower heard about the mess, he was angry with everyone, including himself, that this episode had progressed this far. He told Patton to come to him first in the future if there was a similar problem. Meanwhile, as Patton and Coningham each stood up for his own command, each grudgingly realized that he was impressed with the other's tenacity. American operations had better air cover in the future.

This undeniable tension between the Allies continued. When Alexander planned the final stage of the North African offensive, a direct attack aimed toward the port cities on the Mediterranean coast, the American

forces seemed relegated to a purely supporting role. Even the calm George
Marshall, back in Washington, D.C., became angry when he heard about
this. Patton was convinced that the British troops wanted to preserve all
of the potential glory for themselves. Eisenhower's earlier order that
American commanders not publicly criticize their English counterparts
caused generals like Patton to steam under their helmets. Patton again
took his arguments straight to Alexander, who finally and reluctantly
agreed that American troops could have a greater role in the fighting.

Before this last stage in the North African campaign began, however,
Eisenhower shuffled the commands and Patton was ordered back to his
post in Morocco. Omar Bradley took over command of Second Corps.
Patton had achieved what Ike had wanted him to do: he had restored the
fighting spirit of the men who were beaten at Kasserine and under his
leadership they had gone back into the field and triumphed in combat
over part of the German army. Back in Washington, Chief of Staff Marshall was thrilled with the masterful job Patton had done with the Second
Corps. Frankly, Patton was relieved to be leaving this particular scene, for
his disgust with the political wrangling of the generals had kept growing
the whole time he was there. He had every confidence in Omar Bradley,
who was taking over command of the Second Corps, in part, at Patton's
urgings. Meanwhile, from his headquarters in Morocco, as the Tunisian
campaign ended in success, Patton himself would be taking part in the
planning for the next stage of the war. As in the previous November, in
this next phase Patton would be leading another amphibious assault, this
time on the island of Sicily off the toe of Italy. The operation was code-
named HUSKY, and it would be the first real attack against Adolf Hitler's
"Fortress Europe."

The island of Sicily is roughly triangular with a long flat side to the
north and its third point pulled down to the southeast. It sits just off the
toe of the Italian peninsula. Its strategic position dominates the central
Mediterranean and in 1943 it was seen by most allied planners as the next
logical step toward Europe. Its capture would certainly make an invasion
of Italy much easier, which of course would knock one of the European
Axis powers out of the war.

Much of the planning for HUSKY went on in the Algerian town of Algiers, where Eisenhower now had his headquarters and where British and
American planners went back and forth over different versions and
arrangements. When he was in attendance Patton spent most of his time
watching and listening. He was, in fact, late for the key meeting that set
the plan in motion. Marshall understood that being involved in the de-
liberations was "a poor substitute for active combat," but that if he just

had a little patience, "your turn will soon come again." Patton was not a good waiter, but he could summon up enough patience as long as he believed that bigger things were in store. Marshall's faith in him and reassurance that he would again be needed helped him immeasurably.

Now was one of those times when Patton believed that God had a big plan for him and that belief helped him through his steady conviction that the lion's share of the war plans were still being formulated by the British, for the British. He often remembered how, back in World War I, General Pershing had steadfastly resisted efforts to subordinate the American effort to that of the Allies. He wished there were a Pershing in this war but to no avail. There was not. Neither was there a likelihood that one would emerge, he believed glumly. His British colleagues commanded the air support. General Alexander was still in charge of all the ground forces. Once on Sicily, Montgomery would control the largest port open to the Allies, and Patton would have to make arrangements for all the supplies that would come in earmarked for the American forces. On days when he was moody to begin with, the command arrangements and Eisenhower's appearance of selling out, or being pro-British made him even more depressed. It all boded ill for allied cooperation on Sicily.

Specifically in HUSKY, Patton was going to be in command of the American Seventh Army, coming ashore on the south coast of Sicily. To his army's right, coming in on the east coast of the island, would be General Montgomery commanding the British Eighth Army. The port about which Patton was most concerned, the city of Syracuse, was squarely in the British sector. The plans were set, however, and were not going to be changed just because George Patton was worried about coordinating with Bernard Montgomery over supplies once the armies were across the beaches and firmly fixed in Sicily. Simply getting to that stage would be difficult enough without any extra worries.

As the flagship of the assault force cast off from North Africa on July 6, 1943, Patton was excited to be on the verge of a tremendous battle once again. He had explained to his men as best he could the simple logic of war that so escapes civilians in times of peace. The best and quickest way to win a war once engaged is by destroying the enemy's ability to continue fighting. "To conquer," he told the troops, "we must destroy our enemies. We must not only die gallantly; we must kill devastatingly. The faster and more effectively you kill, the longer will you live to enjoy the priceless fame of conquerors." It was a tough job these soldiers had, and Patton knew it. Tough not only because the Germans and Italians who were dug in on that island over the horizon would fight to their utmost to throw the invading Americans back into the sea, but tough in the philosophical sense that these American boys were not raised to be killing machines. Life was regarded as precious—by many, a gift from God—that was not to be taken lightly. The Biblical injunction against killing, with which so many of Patton's boys had been raised, was not cast aside with thoughtless ease. It took leadership to overcome it in the extreme case of combat and see that these soldiers could steel their hearts and do what was required of them. The old military adage that the only way home was ahead and through the enemy lines certainly held true. "When we land we will meet German and Italian soldiers whom it is our honor and privilege to attack and destroy," he announced after they were underway. "During the last year we Americans have met and defeated the best troops Germany, Italy, and Japan possess. Many of us have shared in these glorious victories. Those of you who have not been so fortunate now have your opportunity to gain equal fame." Patton well knew that fame was the last thing on the average soldier's mind when the bullets began zipping overhead. He knew that glory was a hopelessly remote idea when one was lying shot in a muddy shell hole or bandaged and blinded in an army hospital bed. But he also knew that this kind of performance and exhortation on his part was the only thing that he could do now to light a fire under his boys, and keep their spirits and confidence up, as their boat sailed toward something he knew was utterly unimaginable until they hit the beach, and then get them to fight like men possessed until they did their jobs and everybody could go home again.

Early in the morning of July 10, the soldiers of Patton's Seventh Army began coming ashore along 70 miles of Sicilian beaches. Resistance was light at first but grew heavier throughout the day. Patton himself came ashore on the second morning to survey the action. In and about the town of Gela, right on the coastline and right in the middle of the American landing zone, he found himself in the middle of a German counterattack. It was chaotic. German and American tanks rumbled and squeaked into position to hurl shells at each other. At one point, Patton actually helped some mortar crews sight in their weapons on dug-in German emplacement. German bombers roared over the American positions constantly and bombs crashed down. The building Patton was in suffered a direct hit but was not destroyed. Again he was lucky. "God certainly watched over me today," he wrote in his diary that night.

As the American and British armies gained a foothold and began moving inland, Patton again grew annoyed by the secondary role of his army, ordered to protect the flank and rear of the British. In his own sector, at least, Patton was able to urge his army forward just as fast as it would possibly go and it was having the desired effect. His men were finding abandoned supplies and equipment that should not have been abandoned, and he was proud of how hard they were fighting. They were moving fast: infantry was finding holes in the lines and tanks were then racing through them. Resistance inland at his army's front was crumbling as Italian and German troops moved eastward to stop the British northward thrust toward the city of Messina. Alexander had done an inadequate job of preparing his two commanders to coordinate and cooperate and as a result, Patton and Montgomery often appeared as though they were competing against each other or were just completely ignorant of the other's plans and actions. Alexander even once ordered Montgomery's army to proceed along a road that Patton had already secured and occupied. An entire infantry division had to be moved back to the beaches and then back inland to a new position to let the British use the road.

The Sicilian city of Messina sat right on the narrow band of water separating the island from the mainland of Italy. It was of great strategic significance, for if the allies could take it before all the Germans and Italians got off Sicily, these troops would have no chance of resupply or escape and would eventually have to surrender. Dominating the southern approach to the city, along which the British were fighting, was the towering volcanic cone of Mount Etna. The terrain was difficult for the offensive and much easier for the defensive. Montgomery was soon bogged down and motionless. To break the log-jam, Patton suggested he drive his army to the more lightly defended northern coast, take the city of Palermo up toward the northwest corner, and then approach Messina from the west. Having little other options for restoring forward progress to the operation, Alexander agreed.

On July 23, the city of Palermo fell to the American army. As Patton rode through the streets in his jeep, crowds shouted "Down with Mussolini!" and "Long Live America!" He briefly took over the musty Royal Palace as a headquarters and ordered the German and Italian prisoners of war be used to clean up the streets, the docks, and the harbor. He was treated as a conquering hero and he no doubt loved it. From Washington, President Roosevelt sent his congratulations to Patton along with an autographed picture of the two of them together, taken when FDR visited Casablanca. Winston Churchill telegraphed his warm approval and regard as well. From Eisenhower's headquarters in Algiers, though, there came nothing, only silence. It bothered Patton enough to mention it in a letter to Beatrice.

Despite the regal surroundings, Patton had no intention of staying put for long, because the real target was Messina, even though neither he nor the British had any real plan as to how and by whom it would be captured.

Shortly he received word that one of his infantry divisions had cut through to the northern coast, effectively cutting the island in half. That paved the way for a final push toward Messina, but what was the British army doing now? Were they headed to Messina? Was there going to be another incident about sharing the roads?

The question was answered when Montgomery invited Patton to fly down to his headquarters at Syracuse for a meeting over how the remainder of the campaign would go. The British commanding general had come to realize that he was hopelessly stuck and that Patton's army was the key to getting his moving again. Given the previous situation over roads and supplies, Patton anticipated that Montgomery would behave more like a rival than an ally, and was genuinely surprised (and a little suspicious) when Montgomery suggested that Patton concentrate his forces along the coast road, and to go ahead and capture Messina as soon as he could do so. Patton was even welcome to use the roads in the British sector if he needed.

The fighting along the coast, however, was rough—the toughest of the campaign, in fact. The Germans were contesting every yard of territory and the casualty rates were soaring. The Germans were rigging their own soldiers killed in action with explosives, and some of Patton's men were being maimed and killed by them. As he had consistently done in North Africa, Patton spent time in the hospitals visiting his wounded and handing out any medals or citations that the army had awarded his boys. The sight of men who had lost arms, legs, or eyes really hit him hard. During one visit he pinned 40 Purple Heart medals for being wounded in action on soldiers who had been hit in an air raid. One in particular was unconscious with an oxygen mask over his face. The doctors informed Patton that he would probably not survive his injuries. Nevertheless, Patton knelt down beside the man's bed and pinned the medal on him.

A few days later at a more remote field hospital, Patton called again on some of his wounded. One had the top of his head blown away, a particularly gruesome wound that Patton could hardly bring himself to look at. It was horrible enough that if he were to dwell on it, "I might develop personal feelings about sending men to battle," he confided in his diary. "That would be fatal for a general." Again the doctors explained that here was another who was not going to make it. There were two men who were "completely out from shell shock," he said sadly. "One kept going through the motions of crawling." The doctors told Patton that they were going to give the men tranquilizer shots and they would probably wake up all right. As always, Patton was simultaneously shaken by, and proud of what he found in his hospital visits.

One day while Patton was visiting hospitals, as he moved from bed to bed talking quietly with any of his men who were conscious, he came across a young private, Charles Kuhl, who did not seem to be injured. He was still in uniform and was huddled up on the edge of a bed shivering. Patton had just seen what was called shell shock and this did not look like it. He could see nothing wrong with the man, so he asked what the matter was. "It's my nerves," he said, and started to cry. Patton was thunderstruck and in a flash, lost his temper. He loudly called the man a coward, sprinkled in with other typical profanities, and slapped the soldier on the face, ordering him to stop crying. He turned to the doctors on duty and demanded they remove the man from the tent at once, away from soldiers who were seriously wounded. Patton quickly regained his composure and went about his business. For their part, the doctors were outraged and demanded that "immediate steps be taken to prevent a recurrence of such incidents."

That night, he wrote in his diary that he had met the only errant "coward I have ever seen in this Army." To Patton, this was little different from any other incident in which he felt the need to give a man a jolt to pull him back to an awareness of his duty. He had done just the same, in his judgment, to a soldier back on the beach in Morocco. He had started to do something very similar to a soldier he thought was cowering in a shell hole back during World War I. He had no reason to believe it was not part of his, and the young private's, duty. "I gave him the devil, slapped his face with my gloves, and kicked him out of the hospital." Such men should be dealt with at the company level, not in a hospital, and the problem certainly should not rise through the ranks to come to the attention of higher-ranking officers. If soldiers "shirk their duty, they should be tried for cowardice and shot." The next day he issued an order to all his commanders explaining his concern. The small number of men who let their fear dictate their actions leave their comrades "to endure the dangers of battle while they, themselves, use the hospital as a means of escape." Do not send such men to the hospitals, he ordered. Doing so would only take up beds that should be reserved for the truly wounded.

Patton could not abide such conduct. He demanded bravery under fire from himself, and expected no less from his men. He thought that a failure in this regard was a failure of manhood and was absolute poison to soldiers. It would spread like a forest fire through the ranks. Bravery under fire was a fragile element, despite every appearance of braggadocio or boldness, and a coward could destroy the fighting ability of a group by causing it to doubt its mission, its abilities, and its chances of success.

A week later the scene repeated itself almost exactly. As he moved from bed to bed, there was another private, a young man named Paul Bennett, sitting on a bed shivering. This time it affected Patton even more and, consequently, his reaction was even harsher. He ordered the receiving officer of the hospital not to admit Bennett. "You're a disgrace to the army," Patton seethed, "and you're going back to the front to fight, although that's too good for you. You ought to be lined up against a wall and shot." Patton drew his pistol and shook it at him. He ordered the hospital commander to "get that man out of here right away. I won't have these brave boys seeing such a bastard babied." Patton slapped him twice before the staff steered him away. He stopped at a few more beds and patted a few more shoulders, but all of the wounded soldiers who were conscious had to have been staring wide-eyed at the scene they had all just witnessed. Patton continued to talk, in the main to himself, about cowards and shirkers. His voice full of emotion, he blurted out "I can't help it, but it makes my blood boil to think of a yellow bastard being babied."

After he left the hospital, Patton went to the Second Corps command post where he met Bradley. By now, he had calmed down and saw what had happened as just another job he had had to do. "Sorry to be late, Bradley," he said to his subordinate. "I stopped off at a hospital on the way up." He related what he had seen. "I slapped one of them to make him mad and put some fight back in him." To Patton, that was all he did. Patton later heard word from Bennett's commanding officer that Bennett had been absent without leave and had gone to the hospital after reporting his condition only to the battery surgeon. Patton felt vindicated about his actions. In short order, however, a report came to Bradley's desk from the hospital staff, explaining their take on the whole exchange and demanding that something be done. Bradley, who after all was serving under Patton, chose not to forward the message on to Eisenhower because doing so would disrupt the proper chain of command. He put the message in his desk and closed the drawer.

Ike ended up hearing about the matter anyway, because the doctors who had witnessed both encounters had no such qualms about going over the heads of immediate superiors. When he read their reports, Eisenhower was livid. At the same time, he knew he had to deflect some of the criticism and try to keep the story from blowing up in the press. "If this thing ever gets out," Ike said, "they'll be howling for Patton's scalp, and that will be the end of Georgie's service in this war." Reflecting on what Patton had achieved and what he still could do, he believed that "I simply cannot let that happen. Patton is indispensable to the war effort—one of the guarantors of our victory." On August 17, he sat down and wrote a forceful letter to Patton explaining his position and exactly what he was going to have to do.

The day that Ike wrote that letter, Patton and his troops entered Messina in triumph. A few British soldiers and three tanks joined them, as Montgomery had sent some ahead of the bulk of his forces so that they could take part in the surrender of the city. Even as Patton drove through the filthy, demolished streets in his jeep, German long-range artillery on the Italian mainland across the Strait of Messina lobbed shells into the city. One of the vehicles in Patton's convoy was hit and several men injured. His luck was holding out, but the war was still a long way from being finished.

Just over 80 years earlier, one of Patton's heroes—and one of his grandfather's former professors at VMI—was sitting on a horse at the edge of a devastated battlefield, gazing over the bodies of the soldiers who had given their lives in a desperate attempt to win a closely fought contest. Stonewall Jackson bit into a peach he had earlier picked up off the ground and his pale blue eyes took in the scene of carnage, smoke, and destruction. "God has been very kind to us this day," he said to no one in particular. In the evening after he rode into bombed-out and crumbling Messina like a conquering Roman general, George Patton wrote in his diary as he did most every night. "I feel the Lord has been most generous," he said.

The campaign to take Sicily had been a long and hard fight and had taken the bulk of the summer. From the wreckage of Messina, Patton surveyed the destruction and pondered the cost. He did not realize it at the time, but 40,000 German soldiers and almost twice that many Italians had escaped across the straight to the mainland, along with nearly 50 tanks and 200 artillery pieces. Thousands of American soldiers had lost their lives. Already there was talk of an invasion of Italy. Above all this there still loomed the greatest operation of the war, as allied soldiers would soon have to fight their way onto the northern plain of continental Europe. Patton did not know what his next step would be, where he would go, and what role he would play, but he was ready for it. What he was not ready for, and could not have imagined, was how angry Eisenhower was over the slapping incident and just how many people would now like to see Patton fired, if not court-martialed. If he had had the slightest idea of how close his career was to being over, right now at his moment of triumph, he would have been stunned. He would soon learn.

Chapter 10

EXILE AND REDEMPTION

Grant to our armed forces that disciplined valor and mutual confidence which insures success in war.
Let me not mourn for the men who have died fighting, but rather let me be glad that such heroes have lived.

When Patton opened a letter from Eisenhower on August 20, its energetic condemnation took him completely by surprise. It was in response to the slapping incidents. Ike understood that firm and drastic measures were sometimes needed in order to achieve what had to be done on the battlefield. That did not, however, excuse "brutality, abuse of the sick, nor exhibition of uncontrollable temper in front of subordinates." General John Lucas, Ike's aide who had ferried the letter over from Eisenhower's headquarters in Algiers, met with Patton later that evening to personally explain the depth of his boss' fury. "I feel very low," Patton said after he finally understood.

Ike told Patton that if the stories reaching him were true, he was to seek out and apologize to everyone connected with the whole disgraceful affair. The next day the apologies began, starting with Bennett, the second man Patton had slapped. Patton apologized and they shook hands. The next day he faced the hospital staff and expressed regret for his impulsive actions. At least one of the doctors was unimpressed with Patton's sincerity. The following day, he apologized to Charles Kuhl, the first man he slapped. Kuhl later said graciously that when the incident took place, Patton was probably exhausted and "I think he was suffering a little battle fatigue himself." Over the next week Patton apologized to all of the divisions in his army. He wrote a very heart-felt letter to Eisenhower and apologized for the trouble he had caused his old friend. He thought that would be the end of it. Some days later when the two had lunch together, Patton believed that now every thing was very fine.

The slapping incident nevertheless had a pronounced effect on his career and reputation. Even though Eisenhower resolved not to lose Patton over the mess, he also decided that because of his friend's often-erratic nature, he simply could not be entrusted with overall command of the ground forces in a full-scale invasion of Europe. Patton would never rise higher than command of an army. Later that year, the slapping incident finally broke in the American press. There was an outcry for his immediate removal, and it took the efforts of Chief of Staff Marshall, Secretary Stimson, and again, Eisenhower to convince Patton's detractors, including several representatives and senators, that he was simply indispensable. These three men were Patton's friends, and their friendship served him well at this most crucial point in his career, but these three were also professional military men who understood the qualities a commander simply had to have to be successful. Patton had those qualities and, quite frankly, they were rare. You had to hold on to a person with these qualities, especially in a time of war. The public outcry soon subsided, but not before it cost Patton one of his most treasured possessions. John J. Pershing was shocked and disgusted when he heard of Patton's behavior. It apparently changed for the rest of his life the way Pershing felt about him. Pershing never responded to another one of Patton's letters. Their friendship was over.

Patton remained on Sicily, ensconced at Palermo, awaiting new orders as the tide of the war swept in other directions. The Allies mounted an invasion of Italy that quickly bogged down into stalemate. In September, Patton learned that Omar Bradley had been designated as commander of the U.S. Army for the attack into France across the English Channel, code-named OVERLORD. He took the news hard. Later he learned that Eisenhower had been selected as Supreme Commander of the European invasion force and had moved his headquarters to London. Patton continued to wait for a new assignment, always expecting that one was coming soon. Gradually, however, his certainty about his future began to evaporate. As the weeks turned into months, he began to suspect that perhaps he was, at long last, really finished.

Never did he seem to understand that the root of his exile was his behavior. Eisenhower had exerted every bit of effort he had to keep Patton from being literally fired and shipped back to the states in disgrace, and

Ike was still mad. Patton, however, believed that the pro-British and pro-Allied tendencies of headquarters were the problem. Montgomery got all the credit and all the attention. No one realized the American contribution. No one realized his contribution. He blamed anything at all for his problem except what was really the cause of it: his own behavior. "Georgie is one of the best generals I have," Ike had said to his driver Kay Summersby, "but he's just like a time bomb. You can never be sure when he's going to go off." This was the reason Patton was languishing on Sicily, watching the war pass him by.

While Patton watched the war proceed, the Germans were watching Patton. He was, by their estimation, the most dangerous general the allies had, and they were baffled that he was not in action. There had to be a hidden reason. To capitalize on this and to keep the Germans guessing, Patton traveled around the Mediterranean and allowed himself to be seen and photographed. He went to the island of Corsica and inspected the birthplace of Napoleon. Perhaps he was reconnoitering for an invasion of the southern coast of France, the Germans reasoned. When he turned up in the eastern Mediterranean and in Egypt, it likewise seemed to indicate an invasion of Greece, perhaps. He turned up in Italy to visit troops and take a look at the ongoing stalemate. At the front, a barrage of enemy artillery shells struck just 30 feet from where he stood. It cheered him to be so close to the action again, and, naturally, that his luck was holding up. Nevertheless, he was deeply unimpressed with Mark Clark's leadership of the army. He foresaw continued hard times.

Finally there was a break in the gloom. An order came from the headquarters at Algiers sending Patton to England. England was where the action was, he knew all too well. England was the place from where the grand invasion of the continent was set to embark. Perhaps his future was at last turning around.

Suddenly Patton was in London again. When he called on Eisenhower he finally learned his new position: he was to command the Third Army in the invasion of Europe. He would not be taking part in the actual invasion and that bitterly disappointed him, but once the invading forces established a broad enough base, the Third Army would activate and Patton would be right back in the middle of things. The Third Army, in fact, was not even in England yet; it was still in the United States, but it was on its way over soon. He would be farther from the highest level of operational command than he had become used to, but even that would be all right if he could just get back into the action.

Patton was aghast when he saw how the city had changed since his last visit. There was immeasurable bomb damage everywhere he looked. Kay

Summersby drove him around town and he just could not believe his eyes. His quarters also caused him no small amount of distress. Like all the senior American generals, Patton had an apartment in town. It was decorated like a bordello, he thought, and he could not stand it.

In addition to commanding the Third Army once it was activated, Patton had another, more mysterious role to play in England. Eisenhower and the other OVERLORD planners knew that a colossal build-up of this magnitude simply could not be hidden from spies. The sheer number of ships, vehicles, soldiers, supplies, and support staff made it impossible for the invasion of continental Europe to be unexpected, let alone anything resembling a clandestine operation. The only possible elements of uncertainty that could exist in the minds of the German planners on the receiving end of this attack would be exactly when and where it would be coming. If they could determine that, they could mass sufficient force in the area, first to contain and then repel the invaders. An amphibious attack over a beach is one of the hardest of all military operations to carry out and sustain. The time to defeat the overwhelming numbers and firepower of the Allies then was on the beach. The way to do this was by being prepositioned correctly with sufficient reserves for a massive and decisive counterattack.

How could the Germans figure out where the attack was going to take place? All of southern England was swarming with troops and equipment, with more coming in each week. The capable General Erwin Rommel was now in charge of German coastal defenses from the Netherlands to the western tip of France and he scoured intelligence reports for any possible clues. Gradually German eyes and ears on the ground in England began to see a familiar face. American General George Patton had been spotted in and around London, and increasingly around the southeastern English countryside. Rail and vehicle traffic indicated a substantial concentration in this area. Intelligence reported that an entire army group was being organized in the region. Also, this happened to be the area of England closest to the continent. It was known as the Pas de Calais, and here the English Channel was only a few miles across. It could not be a coincidence. These elements began to convince the German leadership that here was the most likely scene of attack, and Patton, the American general they held in the highest regard, would be its commander.

This is exactly what Eisenhower wanted the Germans to think, because the real attack would instead be coming far to the west, along the coastline of a region of France called Normandy. If the Allies could convince the Germans, however, that the real site was the Pas de Calais, perhaps the landings could be somewhat easier, the initial resistance less, and the

likelihood of success far greater. The Germans might also hold their reserves elsewhere. Ike and his team put together a plan they called FORTI-
TUDE, and it detailed an elaborate deception to mislead the Germans. The
Americans and the British broadcast hours of phony radio transmissions,
coded messages they counted on the Germans to decipher, and deploy-
ment information. They even assembled false tanks and trucks so that
German observation aircraft would see them and report concentrated
equipment.

The centerpiece of the deception, though, was George Patton himself.
Eisenhower was still determined to keep Patton on the sidelines as long as
possible, hoping to avoid any recurring controversies or lingering problems from the incidents in Sicily. FORTITUDE offered a way to both keep
him on the sidelines until later, and also to use his towering reputation as
an asset. Patton traveled around England, meeting local dignitaries and
giving his typical rallying speeches about victory, although now, as there
were civilians and ladies in his audiences, he vowed to tone down the
rampant profanity that was usually part and parcel of these spirited pep
talks.

While giving one of these speeches to an organization in the little town
of Knutsford, Patton again found himself at the center of a whirling controversy. Speaking of the differences that existed between American and
British culture, he quipped that since it was the "evident destiny of the
British and Americans, and, of course, the Russians, to rule the world, the
better we know each other, the better job we will do." It certainly caused
no more than a ripple of applause through the audience. But unknown to
Patton, there was a reporter there, and the next day the newspapers related his speech. Some mentioned that he included the Russians in this
particular remark, but others did not. The next day he received a phone
call from Eisenhower's headquarters asking him to clarify what he had
said. Patton was shocked. He did not have any idea there were correspon-
dents present and had gone out of his way to try to be very careful with his
words.

The crack made little news in England, but the American press jumped
on it. In their initial accounts of the story, most newspapers neglected to
mention that Patton had included the Russians in his original remarks.
Many later ran corrections, but it was too late. Another controversy
erupted. Members of Congress made much of the remarks, demanding
that American officers restrain themselves to fighting the war, not post-
war policy-making and diplomacy. Newspapers that were already in philosophical opposition to Franklin Roosevelt's policies used the story to
criticize the administration's conduct of the war. The whole situation was

made far worse simply by the fact that it was Patton again—the same Patton who had slapped the soldiers back in Sicily.

Eisenhower was upset, primarily because he did not need yet another distraction whose source was George Patton. He admitted to Chief of Staff Marshall that his patience was just about out. Apparently Patton was unable to have any appreciation of the effect that careless remarks or actions could have on public opinion. "I have grown so weary of the trouble he constantly causes you and the War Department," he wrote Marshall, "to say nothing of myself, that I am seriously contemplating the most drastic action."

In retrospect, Eisenhower had so many concerns and worries it seems as though he jumped to the conclusion that this gaff of Patton's was bound to be a controversy on par with the slapping incident. "I have now got all that the army can give me," he told Patton in frustration, and he could not take any more trouble, especially trouble that would deprive him of a fighting Army commander at his time of greatest need. By no means was this affair that serious, however, especially because the initial press stories that had triggered the reaction had related the facts of the story incorrectly. Before he received word back from his superiors at the War Department, Eisenhower was softening his stance. After doing some checking, he realized that Patton's remarks were less offensive than the press had made them out to be. As Marshall reminded Ike of Patton's abilities—a reminder that Eisenhower did not really need—and that they should not be wasted at a time like this, Ike realized that his other commanders simply could not do the job the way Patton could. He would remain in the OVERLORD plan.

In the midst of yet another mess that he had, in part, caused himself, Patton was despondent. He turned down a request to write an article for an American military journal fearing he would inadvertently say something that would get him in more trouble. He thought that "perhaps it would be better if I emulated the owl and just sat and thought." Eisenhower would no doubt agree. Patton took his faithful dog Willie and the two went for a long walk to "see what that does for our self esteem." It had been "a pretty horrid day," he said.

In mid-May there was a big meeting in London in which everyone involved with OVERLORD went over his responsibilities and orders. Everyone from Patton to Eisenhower to Winston Churchill to even King George VI himself was in attendance. At lunch, Patton sat across the table from Churchill who remarkably asked Patton if he happened to remember him. Patton said of course he did. Delighted, Churchill ordered Patton a glass of whiskey. After lunch, Churchill delivered a really great fighting speech, that struck such a chord with Patton he resolved to write a personal letter to Churchill commending him on it. Over the course of the morning and afternoon, the officers in attendance discussed every stage of the operation, leaving nothing to question. It was scheduled to begin early in June.

George Patton's role in the invasion of France was far more than just being a decoy, although in doing what he did, he filled that role perfectly. In the initial wave of the assault across the beaches there would be two American infantry divisions, the First and the Twenty-ninth, along with airborne troops that would parachute or be delivered by glider into Normandy in the dark night hours before the attack. British and Canadian soldiers would simultaneously attack adjacent beaches in the area. The American forces were designated the First Army and were under the command of Omar Bradley. Once all of these Allied forces broke out from the beachhead and began to move across open country, the Third Army under Patton's command would be activated, General Courtney Hodges would assume command of First Army, and Bradley would bump up to army group commander over both of these individual armies. When Patton took charge of Third Army in preparation for action, Third Army strength was over 200,000 men and 40,000 vehicles organized into 13 divisions, both infantry and armored.

Just a few days before the invasion was to begin, Montgomery, Bradley, and Patton had dinner together at Montgomery's headquarters near Portsmouth on the southern coast of England and talked through everything one last time. Patton was frankly a little worried that his army would have little to do once the First Army achieved the breakout and, at least theoretically, had the Germans on the run. Bradley and his staff might not have minded if that situation had arisen, for most of them had little use for Patton and his antics. Montgomery, on the other hand, seemed most interested in using Patton and his army just as much as circumstances would allow. Since Patton and Bradley had planned to spend the night, the three generals talked long into the evening. The next morning at breakfast Patton came to believe that he and "Monty" finally were beginning to understand each other.

In the weeks before the invasion, Patton traveled from corps to corps and division to division giving a rousing pep talk to the soldiers for which he soon became famous. He was captivating, inspiring, energizing, and theatrical. His men loved it. Sometimes his high-pitched voice surprised those who had not heard him speak before, especially those who happened to be in the front row of the crowd who got a good look at the scowl before he began speaking. He touched on everything from pride and patriotism to duty and courage. The men hung on his every word. He spoke softly and he shouted. Peppered throughout each of his speeches was more profanity than most people were used to hearing in a week, but his troops loved it and laughed, cheered, and yelled. Always there was the Patton stamp of action, action, and more action. Always keep moving forward, he demanded. The tougher the attack, the quicker they would all get home. "We want this thing over with," he acknowledged to his men. "But you can't win a war lying down. The quickest way to get it over with is to get the bastards. The quicker they are whipped, the quicker we go home. The shortest way home is through Berlin!" The troops roared their approval. They believed every word of it mainly because Patton himself believed every word of it.

On the morning of June 6, the invasion began. Patton heard news of it at his headquarters near the town of Knutsford on the BBC radio broadcasts. The waiting was tough on him and to pass the time, he wrote to his son, who was then a cadet at the Military Academy at West Point. "I have no immediate idea of being killed but one can never tell and none of us can live for ever so if I should go, don't worry but set your self to do better than I have." He did not know for sure yet when Eisenhower would call for him and his men. "It is Hell to be on the side lines and see all the glory eluding me, but I guess there will be enough for all," he wrote to his wife after writing his son. The fighting had been going on across the Channel for less than a day and already his anticipation and impatience was evident. "I guess I will read the Bible," he said.

Day after day after day Patton sat and waited. News trickled back from Normandy, sometimes good, sometimes not so good. It seemed almost from hour to hour word changed from the attack being stalled out, to it making good progress. And then it was back to being stopped. To pass the time, he studied maps in anticipation, and read books on the Normandy and Brittany campaigns of William the Conqueror, almost 1,000 years earlier. He anticipated using many of the same roads and routes that William had used and marked up his maps with strategic notes and reminders to himself. One night to fight his jittery boredom, he went to the theater in nearby Manchester. After the play, the leading man announced that the one and only U.S. Army General George S. Patton was in the audience and the whole theater burst into cheers. He went back stage to meet the cast and when he came out to his car, there was still a huge crowd waiting for him. "I had a hell of a time keeping it out of the papers," he explained to Beatrice. It all lifted his emotions, but he could not escape the feeling he belonged elsewhere. Just across the Channel in northern

France, the battle was still raging, and Patton could not sit still for long when that was the case. He could almost hear the guns.

Finally at the end of June he began to shift from command post to command post, always moving southward toward the coast. On July 6, exactly one month after the invasion began, Patton boarded a cargo transport plane and, with an escort of four fighter planes, flew over to France. One of Bradley's aides met them at a landing strip near one of the beaches. As he was briefed on the progress, it became painfully clear that the operation was not nearly as far along as had been originally hoped. Montgomery's British forces had yet to take a crucial town that he had initially anticipated taking on day one. Over one million allied fighting men were now in northern France, but progress had all but stopped.

To break the stalemate, Bradley came up with a daring plan to use intensive bombing from the air along with strong concentrations of tanks to punch a hole through the German lines. Summer rains caused the plan to be delayed. Before he knew it, Patton had been in France over three weeks and had seen no combat. Finally on July 25 and 26, thousands of bombs rained down on the enemy lines. Some went tragically awry and hit American troops. Hundreds were killed and wounded, included one high ranking general, Lesley McNair, one of Patton's good friends. "A sad ending and a useless sacrifice," Patton said after a small handful of officers gathered quietly to lay their friend to rest in the fields of France.

Even though it was not immediately obvious, the bombing operation was a huge success. American forces found a hole in the German lines and three whole divisions poured through. Six days later, at noon on August 1, Patton's Third Army became operational.

The days of stalemate were over. When the American forces broke through the lines, they opened a period of racing, mobile warfare never surpassed in modern military history. Patton was on the go all the time, often chasing after his divisions as they spread out through northeastern France. As was his way, it seemed he magically appeared at every point where something had gone wrong. Sometimes he came upon troops being held up by German fire. When this happened, he quickly found the commander and convinced him to keep trying different tactics until something worked. At the western end of the allied lines, there were two small towns, Avranches and Pontaubault. Patton intended to take his divisions through these two towns, around the end of the line, and then he would be loose in France. The potential for endless traffic jams in this narrow bottleneck, though, was substantial. At one point, he came across a gridlocked intersection in Avranches. He angrily climbed to the top of a covered police box and for an hour and a half directed traffic like a police officer in a busy city. Somehow Patton and his men got all his tanks, trucks and soldiers through on a narrow two-lane road without a hitch. This in itself was a tremendous achievement.

Over past the western end of the allied lines, German resistance was beginning to disintegrate. Patton sent two armored divisions racing westward into the Brittany peninsula to secure some cities and try to pin down and isolate the remaining German forces in the region. Sometimes these divisions moved so fast Patton and his headquarters actually lost track of them. Other times, Patton would walk along with infantry divisions, encouraging them, and urging them to press on faster. Patton's point was simple: now that they had achieved the long-awaited breakout, under no circumstances should they pause to let the Germans regroup. The Americans had the upper hand and the Germans were reeling. Now was not the time to worry about open flanks; now was the time to take advantage of the enemy's disorganization, keep him off balance, and press him until he collapsed. Doing this would defeat Germany sooner. Doing this would end the war sooner. "We want this thing over with," he had told his men back in England. "The quicker they are whipped, the quicker we go home." He had meant it then and now he saw the way to bring it about.

With a boldness bordering on recklessness, Patton wanted to run like a dog in a field of birds and in effect chase the Germans all the way back into Germany if he could not surround them and cut them off first. By the end of its first week of operation, Patton's Third Army had driven the Germans out of almost 120 towns and villages and had liberated over three million people. His army was starting to cover so much ground he had to fly in a small airplane to go from one corps and one division to the next. He hated it. He would much rather be on the ground. There was German anti-aircraft artillery all over. "I feel like a clay pigeon," he said.

By no means was it all racing and no fighting. On the contrary, there was fighting going on constantly somewhere in Third Army's area of operations. As a measure of the resistance Patton was facing, in just over two weeks his men had killed somewhere around 10,000 German soldiers in battle. Also by his count, they had captured about 47,000 of the enemy. Just like in Sicily, he could tell by the amount of equipment the Germans were leaving behind just how frantic their retreat was becoming. He credited the success he was having to his decision to "cut the armored divisions loose" and "not tie them to the infantry." His tanks were running over the French countryside like the cavalry of days gone by. He loved it.

Part of Patton's tremendous run of success in the late summer of 1944 was his personal drive and his determined leadership. He pushed his men to their very limit without letting up at all. But another part of the equation was something much more clinical and, in a sense, formulaic. Patton and his Third Army were at the precise place at the precise time to see an age-old military principle at work. If a fighting force can turn its opponent's flank—if it can get around to an open end of the line—it can then turn 90 degrees and roll right up the line. The opponent can then try to reorient its front, turn itself 90 degrees, and then try to continue the fight, or it can pull back and set up a new defensive line somewhere in the rear.

Patton's real contribution came not in turning the German positions then, but by the ferocity of his pursuit. Rather than give the Germans any time to set up a new defense, Patton insisted that if his army simply stayed on the move, always skirting around wherever the Germans might try to draw up a new defense, they would never be able to do so. A fast-running pursuit would deny the Germans even the chance of turning and fighting. Any enemy unit that did turn and fight would risk being cut off from the others and forced to surrender. This was a job for the cavalry. The dashing, saber-wielding horsemen would come charging in as soon as an opening emerged and the opponent would crumble and turn in headlong retreat. The horses and riders would give chase, never allowing the enemy to reassemble to put up resistance. It happened this way back in 1861 in Northern Virginia at the First Battle of Manassas. The invading Federal army did not stop running until it crossed the Potomac. It could happen that way again here in 1944. George Patton was still a hard-riding cavalryman. The only thing that had changed was that now he was sitting in a tank instead of in a saddle.

As he charged across France, Patton's superiors worried about his open right flank down south. If enemy forces were to somehow turn Patton's right end with sufficient numbers, the whole allied force might have to come to a stop. Patton, however, was not worried. He had found a new way to cover his dashing open flank. General Otto P. Weyland was commander of the tactical air forces that were attacking the Germans from the air in the summer of 1944. Weyland was loyal to Patton and the Third Army and was ready to provide whatever service he could. "The Air Force takes care of my flanks," Patton explained when asked if he was worried about them. At one point, 20,000 German soldiers surrendered to a small group of infantry just to avoid being attacked from the air again. "You guard the right flank. I can't be bothered," he told Weyland. If there was any German force trying to creep around to the edge of Patton's army, "you hit it with air and watch it; we are going straight east."

As Third Army turned to race east, Patton and his staff kept a running total of their own casualties and those they had caused. There was really no comparison. By August 26, the imbalance was clear, and it spoke to the drive and abilities of the men. Third Army had killed 16,000 Germans at a cost of 1,930 of its own. It had taken 65,000 prisoners and had only 1,854 of its own missing in combat. In every town, the citizens came out to cheer the Americans. Patton was at the same time joyous and glum. He relished the role of the conquering liberator. There was nothing else like it and it suited him perfectly. All the while, however, he kept his eye on the future. "It will be pretty grim after the war to drive ones self and not be cheered but one gets used to anything," he wrote.

One of the most controversial decisions of the war was Omar Bradley's order for Patton to stop a possible swing northward in hopes of catching an entire German army that had launched a last-ditch attack back toward the town of Avranches. Canadian soldiers were having a tough time pushing southward and a possible link-up with Third Army, thereby trapping the Germans, was growing less likely by the hour. Patton announced that he could still continue northward and the trap could still be sprung. But everything was happening too fast for Bradley. He ordered Patton to stop. Later he explained that he feared that the Third Army and the Canadians could have a deadly meeting with friendly-fire casualties before recognizing each other. It was another several days before the Allied armies closed the gap.

Perhaps surprisingly, Patton did not seem too distressed about the missed opportunity. Both he and Montgomery were far more interested in a longer envelopment, all the way to the Seine River, that would prevent an entire German Army group from escaping back to Germany. The Germans kept retreating, however, and the Americans kept chasing. Some of Patton's men were the first allied troops to cross the Seine, but a French army was allowed to liberate Paris. Incredibly, by the end of August, the Third Army was all the way across France and entering into the battlefields of World War I. German resistance was negligible.

There was trouble brewing, though, borne of this tremendous success. On August 28, Patton wrote that "at the present time, my chief difficulty is not the Germans but gasoline." The Third Army, which needed 350,000 gallons of gasoline a day in its dash across France, was beginning to outrun its supply lines. "If they would just give me enough gas," he knew he could get anywhere with his army he wanted to go. The next day, however, he found out that his army was 140,000 gallons short.

As the Allied armies closed in on the German border, Eisenhower had a tough decision to make. Should the advance proceed along a broad front, allowing for all the allied fighting forces to enter Germany, or should there be a narrower, deeper push toward some kind of specific target? Montgomery's armies in the north were not moving as far as Patton's but there were particularly important targets in his path that had a political aspect. Namely, there were the launching pads for Hitler's V-2 rockets that were hitting London packed with explosives. There was little chance that these terror weapons could have any appreciable effect on the outcome of the war, but Churchill wanted them taken out of action as soon as possible.

Another difficulty aggravated the supply problem. Even though the British forces had captured the crucial port city of Antwerp, Belgium, they had not secured the estuary that led from the sea to the port. Consequently, Antwerp could not yet be used for supply. Largely because of this, the supply situation in Northern France for the allies was horrible. Patton's army, for instance, was literally hundreds of miles from the only ports into which were flowing all of the supplies it needed, from gasoline to ammunition. One hundred days into the fighting, Patton's army was already where planners had not expected it to be until May 1945. There was no way that all the armies could keep up a broad front strategy. Back in Normandy, there were plenty of supplies—an abundance of all kinds, even gasoline. The problem was getting it all to the front.

Patton suspected that Eisenhower was again favoring the British over the Americans and he was not pleased with the situation. And in this case, however, Patton was correct. While Montgomery hacked ahead into Belgium, the Third Army was ordered to hold its position. Even Bradley, one step up the chain of command from Patton, was annoyed. Patton could sense that the Germans he had been chasing since he came to France were beginning to dig in to stop him. "Look at the map!" he said. The German plain stretched out before him with little chance for a defensive stand by an army on the run. "If I could only steal some gas, I could win this war." He was irritated that Ike kept talking about "the future great battle of Germany, while we assured him that the Germans will have nothing left to fight with if we push on now. If we wait," he added, "there will be a great battle of Germany." He would have to wait, though. Gasoline was just too scarce. Monty's forces had first priority. Supply problems were achieving all that the enemy had not been able to achieve.

Patton's men tried every trick in the book to divert as much fuel as possible from Montgomery's First Army to the Third Army. From time to time he felt like there must be a conspiracy to deny him victory, but most of the time he saw things clearly. The supply officer "has done an amazing job" he finally admitted, and accepted the fact that he would no longer be moving as much as he would like.

For the rest of the autumn, as the rains began to fall, Patton's army crept forward only slowly. He laid siege to a series of forts around the old town of Metz. The fighting was becoming more like that of World War I now, he said. Not until November was Metz cleared of German troops. One day he was visiting hospitals, which he had continued to do once he was back in command, and he asked a wounded soldier who had taken part in the fighting if he had heard that Metz had finally fallen. The soldier admitted that he had. Patton took him by the hand and smiled. "Tomorrow, son, the headlines will read 'Patton Took Metz,' which you know is a...lie. You and your buddies are the ones who actually took Metz." Such was the kind of quiet pep talk that he delivered so often that made him so popular with most of his men. Others never heard it.

Supplies were not the only resource hard to come by. When Patton went to hospitals to visit the men, he knew full well that until they got back on the field, the Third Army would not be at full strength. Replacements were almost impossible to get. By the end of November, the army was 9,000 short on replacements. "I cannot see why Eisenhower could be caught short on both men and ammunition, because after all, these are the two elements with which wars are fought." He planned to turn some of his headquarters staff into infantrymen just to help make up part of the shortfall in the ranks. A few days later, he was 11,000 short.

As the weather turned colder, Patton and the Third Army spent most of their time sitting and waiting. There was sporadic fighting but no more big moves, no more big attacks. It seemed as though the war was about to bog down for the winter. A cold rain continued into December. He and his men had pushed about 40 miles through a series of defended towns until the army was up against the German border. Now from across that border were coming little clues that the German army might be up to something. Lots of trains were reported to be coming and going. To the north of his sector, tank and infantry divisions were said to be gathering. On the cold, clear night of December 14, the unmistakable sound of tanks squeaking along, carried through the Ardennes forest as Patton's men peered into the darkness from their foxholes, watching for any sign of movement. Until—and unless—something happened, though, Patton intended to push his supply-short army forward as much as he could. He and his staff began putting together a plan for an offensive to be launched on December 19. On the foggy morning of December 16, that plan had to be shelved.

Chapter 11
FINISHING THE JOB

Strengthen my soul so that the weakening instinct of self-preservation, which besets all of us in battle, shall not blind me to my duty, to my own manhood, to the glory of my calling, and to my responsibility to my fellow soldiers.

Before the sun rose on Saturday, December 16, 1944, American soldiers hunkered down in their foxholes in the dense and snowy Ardennes forest miles north of George Patton's Third Army experienced one of the most sustained and heavy artillery attacks the Germans had ever put together. Most of the soldiers were dug in well enough to weather the roaring and flashing blast, but just its fury alone was surprising and unnerving. As the sun began to lighten the eastern sky, however, it became clear that more trouble was on the way. On the hilltops to the east were assembled more German tanks and guns than the Americans had seen in one place in months. At the same time, scattered American patrols out in the woods spotted long columns of German infantry on the march, heading toward the front lines. The Americans in their front line foxholes put up a tough fight, but the numbers coming at them, backed by tanks and artillery, were simply too much. Some began to pull back. Others realized only too late that they were surrounded, having fought on until they ran out of ammunition. The rest lay dead in their foxholes, still in their positions.

Army Group commander Omar Bradley, who at the time of the attack was meeting with Eisenhower at his headquarters far behind the front lines, figured that this was nothing more than an attack designed primarily to force Patton to divert some of his troops northward to take the heat off the German forces that were stubbornly holding up the Third Army's progress. "A spoiling attack," he called it. Ike, however, thought differently. He had been worried about several weak sectors in the allied lines for quite a while now, and this German attack had hit precisely one of these weakened sectors. Ike ordered Bradley to transfer a couple of armored divisions from Patton's army northward to help hold off the Germans. They both knew that Patton would not like this, but Eisenhower, worried about the severity of the attack, held fast. Bradley headed to Patton's headquarters in the town of Nancy to explain the situation.

Patton clearly understood what was happening as he and Bradley looked over the maps. There was an enormous westward bulge in the allied lines where the Germans were attacking. The lines had not broken, though, at least not yet. The southern shoulder of the bulge was just north of the Third Army, and Patton told Bradley that he would immediately break off his movement eastward and get ready to redirect his entire force 90 degrees to the left for a thrust into the southern flank of the German advance. He and his staff quickly worked out all the details before Patton left for Verdun and a big meeting of most of the major allied commanders. He anticipated that Ike would call on him to start his troops moving as soon as possible and he wanted to be one step ahead of his boss. Before he left, he agreed that he would telephone his staff from Verdun when the final decision was reached and say a specific code that would indicate exactly which of his forces would need to move, and the precise route they would take northward.

Patton was excited about the possibilities this German offensive opened up. After his progress had dwindled to a crawl, he had feared that the war would drag on and become like the first war he had fought near this very same ground. Now, however, the Germans had come out of their holes and trenches into the open. The Americans could smash them now like they had back in the summer. The situation could hardly have been more advantageous, although things looked bad right now. This attack, Patton thought, could end up being the last gasp of the German army. After he got through with them, they would have nothing left.

Eisenhower was clearly tense when he arrived at Verdun, but he was grimly determined to turn the situation to the advantage of the Allies. Patton on the other hand was more openly energetic and confident. He was wearing his best war face and chomping on a cigar as the commanders gathered around a small stove for heat in an old French barracks. Everyone agreed that all other offensive operations had to stop until their forces could contain this breakout. "The present situation is to be re-

garded as one of opportunity for us and not of disaster," Eisenhower announced. Shortly he turned his attention to Patton and his forces, the un-
engaged troops who were closest to the bulge. When could he bring six
divisions together and attack?

Patton calmly announced that in three days he could attack with three
divisions. It was a bold announcement and was received as such by those
in attendance. It caused quite a commotion, he thought. He was quite
pleased with the reaction. To be able to do this in three days was indeed a
feat of notable generalship. Eisenhower worried, however, that despite the
rapidity with which the blow could be struck, three divisions was not
enough force. He wanted the bulging salient crushed, not dented, and he
wanted six divisions to make sure the job was done right. Patton believed
that three were enough, and true to his inherent cavalry commander's
dash and boldness, he knew that the longer he waited, the less would be
the element of surprise and shock to the Germans. This was a time for
bold and quick action. This was a time for audacity. Sensing that Ike was
going to stick hard on the call for six divisions, Patton agreed to reinforce
his initial attack within a week. With this assurance, Eisenhower gave
him the green light. Patton walked to the telephone and made a call back
to his headquarters. Thousands of tanks and other vehicles began turning
north and heading in the direction of a little crossroads town in Luxembourg called Bastogne.

Bastogne turned out to be an important town for the German advance
because of the way it dominated the road network through the region.
There in the little town of 4,000 residents, elements of the 101st Airborne
Division had dug themselves in and refused to retreat. By Thursday, December 21, the day before Patton would be attacking northward with his
three divisions, they realized they were surrounded. German forces had
cut off every road. Like army units of old, they formed a defensive circle
and waited for the cavalry to come. They did not know when it would
come, or if it would come at all, but they were determined to hold out.

On December 22, the Germans surrounding Bastogne sent in to town,
under a flag of truce, a note requesting that the defenders surrender. The
American commander, Anthony McAuliffe, entered into military history
with his infamous one-word response. "To the German Commander:" he
wrote. "Nuts!" He signed the typed note "The American Commander."
The next day was the first since the attack began on which the skies were
clear and over 240 cargo planes dropped ammunition and supplies to the
surrounded men. Still, the artillery that was present had to ration its
shells. No one knew when such a resupply airlift could occur. On the afternoon of Christmas Eve, a message came in from corps headquarters. It

was from George Patton. "Christmas Eve present coming up," it said. "Hold on."

At the head of the cavalry bound for Bastogne was the Fourth Armored Division and at Patton's order the tanks were in the lead. Patton had originally been irritated that the 101st had been left in Bastogne, and his goal in driving northward was nothing more than to smash into the German flank, cut through it completely, reestablish a straight and unbroken front, and surround the elements of the entire German offensive. He did not conceive of what he was doing as primarily a rescue mission. If he could lift the siege at Bastogne in addition to destroying the Germans, well, that would be fine. When one of his Generals, VIII Corps commander Troy Middleton, pointed out using a detailed map just how much a key position Bastogne really was, Patton began to understand the need to hold it. Relieving the 101st became a higher priority.

There was almost no chance at all, however, for Patton's divisions to reach the 101st on Christmas day, so in that sense, his dispatch to McAuliffe forwarded through headquarters was a bit misleading. Patton knew the importance of morale, though, and wanted the defenders to know he was on his way. Morale was important for his own troops, of course, and he spent every waking minute out among them. On Christmas day, he tried to ensure that every soldier in his army got a hot turkey dinner. Even though it was unbelievably cold, Patton spent hour after hour in an open jeep, going from unit to unit. Very often, the columns would begin cheering as he zipped alongside them, arms folded across his chest, his war face firmly—often frozen, probably—in place. Once when he came upon a vehicle that had slid off an icy road, he ordered his jeep to stop. He jumped out and began pushing and yelling and cursing along with the soldiers. "He yelled to us to get out and push," one of the soldiers involved remembered, "and first I knew, there was General Patton pushing right alongside of me."

He still had his gruff and uncompromising way about him and he still had the capacity to fly off the handle when he felt a soldier was shirking his duty. More than once he loudly berated soldiers for cowardice. He tended to have little patience for, or interest in, anything that was going on in and around the army that was not directly related to him or what he was pushing his troops to do. Although if something that displeased him caught his attention, he could easily explode. Once he sent for journalist and cartoonist Bill Maudlin whose comic about scruffy tired soldiers was a regular and popular feature in the army's *Stars and Stripes* newspaper. Patton hated it, believing that it ruined morale, and let Maudlin have it for 45 minutes. "The krauts ought to pin a medal on you," he ranted angrily.

Patton demanded he stop drawing such a denigrating cartoon. Maudlin kept drawing. The next year he won a Pulitzer Prize for his work and one of his cartoon soldiers appeared on the cover of *Time* magazine.

Sometimes, though, Patton could tell when he had pushed too far. When a German counterattack against one of his corps resulted in heavy losses, he understood that he was partly to blame. "It is probably my fault, because I had been insisting on day and night attacks. This is alright on the first or second day of battle and when we had the enemy surprised, but after that the men get too tired." On December 26, the lead elements of the Fourth Armored Division finally broke through to Bastogne. The bulge in the lines was finally cut off and the Germans in it isolated by the end of January.

The American press, even though it had jumped on Patton relentlessly during the controversy over the slappings on Sicily and had eagerly lambasted Patton over his inappropriate remarks in England, were at once back in his corner during the Battle of the Bulge. The *Washington Post* reported that "when there is a fire to be put out, it is Patton who jumps into his boots, slides down the pole, and starts rolling." Winston Churchill said the entire operation was "the greatest American battle of the war," and even the German commander Von Rundstedt, who was captured after the war, told his captors that "Patton, he is your best." The victory was a costly one, however. In Patton's Third Army, almost 4,500 soldiers were killed in battle between December 22 and January 29. Over 20,000 were wounded.

Patton was horribly disappointed by the lack of progress early in 1945 after the Battle of the Bulge. Even though he figured that the German army had to be exhausted now, he was only permitted to resume the same slow, creeping forward movement of his army that had characterized the previous autumn's campaign. Eisenhower approved in theory the idea of a single thrust toward Berlin rather than the broad front, but he also wanted all of his commanders to move forward and close to the Rhine River. "There are too many 'safety first' people" running the war, Patton complained. It wasn't just Patton by himself this time. Army group commander Omar Bradley was growing disgusted, too. When Bradley found out that the Combined Chiefs of Staff was planning to take some divisions from his armies to form a "theater reserve" he exploded. Patton, who was in the room when this happened, had never seen Bradley lose his temper and get so angry. "Tell them we will all resign," Patton yelled as Bradley argued over the telephone with headquarters. For one last time in the war, Patton and Bradley were standing together again. Patton called the theater reserve plan "locking the door after the horse was stolen." As far as he could judge, the need for a reserve had passed. The Germans had done all they could do. They were beaten. He could prove it, and in so doing end the war, he thought, if Ike would just turn him loose.

To make matters more frustrating, by February General Montgomery was putting pressure on Eisenhower to shift control of the American Tenth Army to his control. Montgomery fully intended to make sure that the British were the first across the Rhine River. Ike agreed with Monty's requirements only with the provision that Bradley's army group shift northward to take over the space of the American Tenth. Montgomery dropped the matter. "Damn this political war," Patton wrote in his diary.

The supply situation was better now, but that made his active defense orders even more distasteful. The Rhine River was now the last major barrier between the Allies and Germany, and Patton started worrying that unless they all moved quickly, the Germans could retreat behind it, blow up all its bridges, and decimate the Americans and British as they tried to cross it. Eisenhower had given a green light to a steady approach to the river by all the American forces all along the front, and even though his subordinate generals often figured otherwise, Eisenhower had no intention of letting Montgomery's advance be the only one for the Allies. He wanted multiple advances to guarantee the success of at least one. Patton, Bradley, and many other American commanders by this time nursed a strong desire to beat Montgomery across the river. "I will be the first on the Rhine yet," Patton privately vowed.

Patton's staff had been planning the crossing for months and even though events now began to move quickly, there was no recklessness. The Third Army approached the Rhine along ancient roads through the old city of Trier. He knew very well that the legions of Julius Caesar had used this same route during Caesar's campaigns in Gaul and he was delighted to be doing the same, thousands of years later. As he prepared to take the town, he reread Caesar's *Gallic Wars* commentary. "It is interesting to view in imagination the Roman legions marching down that same road," he said. He could "smell the sweat of the legions."

As the Third Army finally approached the Rhine, the biggest problem was that there were no intact bridges in its sector. But Patton feared that if he did not get his men across the river quickly, headquarters might take divisions from him and give them to Montgomery or maybe to the American First Army and General Courtney Hodges, who had become somewhat of a rival to Patton. Hodges had already pushed several divisions across the Rhine at the town of Remagen in tough fighting and had little patience with Patton and his bombastic hi-jinks. To get his own force across the Rhine would ensure its continued use, Patton believed, and so he was determined to do it. He consistently pushed his forces ahead just a little bit beyond his specific orders. On the morning of March 23, the telephone rang in Bradley's office. It was Patton. "Brad, don't tell anyone, but I'm across," he told him. "Well, I'll be damned," Bradley said. "You mean across the Rhine?" Patton did not want the Germans to know of his exploit until he got as many divisions across as he could, but once the Germans found out, Patton immediately wanted the whole world, especially Montgomery, to know the Third Army was already across the Rhine.

Although Patton often thought that he was getting away with more than headquarters wanted him to do, Ike almost always knew very well what Patton was up to, and his old friend continued to please him, even though he sometimes could not come right out and say it. He appreciated Patton's drive, dedication, and results. "You have made your Army a fighting force that is not excelled in effectiveness by any other of equal size in the world, and I am very proud of the fact that you, as one of the fighting commanders who has been with me from the beginning of the African campaign, have performed so brilliantly throughout." When Eisenhower forwarded Patton a copy of a congratulatory message Chief of Staff Marshall had sent him, Ike wrote his own note to Patton at the bottom. "I continue to have reason to cheer that you came with me to this war. Always, Ike."

At about 10:00 P.M. on the night of March 22, the first of Patton's troops had begun ferrying across the Rhine River. Soon he had a whole division across. The day after he related the news to Bradley, Patton himself walked across on a pontoon bridge. He was delighted and proud of his men. "The highest honor I have ever attained is that of having my name coupled with yours in these great events," he told his troops. That same day he crossed the Rhine, the Third Army took its 300,000th German prisoner since August 1. "I do not see how they can keep it up much longer," he wrote.

Almost as soon as he got across the Rhine, however, Patton created more trouble for himself. He received some intelligence that his son-in-law, Lieutenant Colonel John Waters, his older daughter's husband, who had been captured by the Germans two years earlier, might be in a prison camp at the nearby town of Hammelburg, just 60 miles away. Inspired by a similar mission that Douglas MacArthur had put together in the Philippines a month before that resulted in about 5,000 prisoners and civilians liberated, Patton assembled a small task force to raid the prison camp and free those held inside, among whom he hoped was his son-in-law. Sixteen tanks, 27 trucks, and almost 300 men and officers took part. It was a dangerous gamble and Patton knew it. "I have been nervous as a cat all day as every one but me thought it too great a risk. I hope it works."

The force crashed through the camp gates and liberated several thousand prisoners, but in the resulting fight, the attackers were severely shot up and many of the prisoners, too, were seriously wounded. Three German divisions then moved in and surrounded the elements of the task force and destroyed it. Almost everyone involved was wounded, dead, or captured. It was a disastrous and foolhardy operation. Waters, who indeed had been there, was among those shot in the confusion and was taken to an evacuation hospital in Frankfurt. Patton traveled to see him and pinned the Silver Star for valor on his son-in-law.

Eisenhower angrily called it the latest of Patton's crackpot actions. "I took Patton's hide off," over the matter he assured General Marshall. All that kept it from becoming another full-blown public relations disaster was the sudden death of President Roosevelt that occurred at about the same time. In terms of judgment, it was one of Patton's worst moments, on a par with the slapping incident.

In April, Patton, Eisenhower, Bradley, and other commanders went to see the Ohrdruf concentration camp that the Fourth Armored Division had recently liberated. The guards had fled before the camp fell, but not until they had murdered every one of the prisoners. There were bodies everywhere. Some had starved to death; some had been burned. Patton was so disgusted he became physically sick beside one of the buildings. More and still greater disgust was in store when the Third Army came across the Buchenwald extermination camp. Again Patton was made ill by the sights and smells. He suggested that Ike send in photographers and the press to see the full ghastly spectacle. In a letter, Patton wrote "honestly, words are inadequate to express the horror of these institutions." Eisenhower himself inspected each of these camps, he said, "in order to be in a position to give first-hand evidence of these things if ever, in the future, there develops a tendency to charge these allegations merely to 'propaganda.'" Ike ordered the American soldiers not in the front lines to be brought up to tour the camps so they would know exactly what they were fighting for. For his part, Patton always ordered the local townspeople to dig the graves and bury the corpses of such camps as the Third Army encountered. He ordered the 1,500 most prominent citizens of the nearby town of Weimar to be marched through the camp "and made to look at the horrid spectacle. I do not believe that even the Germans realized to what depths they had sunk."

It was just about this same time that the American high command began to make the initial arrangements regarding the ultimate liberation of the German capital of Berlin. Eisenhower informed Patton and Bradley of a line along the Elbe River at which the Americans and the British would halt to allow the Soviet Red Army to take Berlin. Patton was stunned and disappointed at the decision, but was calm about it. "We had better take Berlin, and quick" he urged Ike, along with the rest of Germany over to its eastern border. The Allies could be to Berlin in two days, he told his old friend. "Well, who would want it?" Patton's aide Hobart Gay remembered Eisenhower asking. Patton put his hands on Ike's shoulders. "I think history will answer that question for you."

By the end of April, the war was almost over. As anyone who has long anticipated a big event knows, once whatever it is happens, there is always somewhat of a letdown. Many times there is not the big, sudden rush of elation we anticipate ushering in some long-awaited, hard-fought success. Sometimes there is just quiet fatigue. This is how it was for George Patton. "The war is sort of petering out," he wrote at the end of April. "We can go anywhere we want with very limited opposition." He was growing convinced that American forces were in for "a non-spectacular termination" despite rumors swirling around that Hitler was dead and that the Germans were about to make an official surrender. Hitler committed suicide on April 30.

Nearing the end of this most strenuous but satisfying time of his life, Patton began to sink into depression. The enemy troops in his sector "will quit to day or tomorrow," he wrote Beatrice, "and I will be out of a job. I feel lower than whale tracks on the bottom of the ocean." He could not imagine what his future would be after the war ended. "Peace is going to be hell on me," he told her. His glum nature sometimes led him to think that his life was running a parallel course with the war—maybe they would be ending at the same time. Over his years he had come close to death many times and in each instance had come through, but maybe now his time was just about done. Maybe he had now done what he was here to do. "Sometimes I feel that I may be nearing the end of this life," he wrote her. "Well, if I do get it," he said, speaking of death, "remember that I love you." This morose tone did not continue through many of his letters and writings during this time, but a kind of weariness was clearly evident. "I would like to come home for at least a few days," he wrote to Beatrice later, "I miss you." Germany surrendered to the Allies on May 7.

Patton hoped that he could be transferred to the Pacific Theater of Operations to fight Japan. It was clear that in Europe, the American army was going to be acting as an army of occupation, and he had little desire or capacity for being a good post-war administrator-general. Germany was utterly destroyed and while Patton had no pity for the soldiers and leaders who had caused the war in the first place, the conditions in which many of the German civilians had to live depressed him terribly. Most of the people he saw were old men, women or children, and in the towns and cities, most of them lived in the dank basements of bombed-out buildings. He felt that the German nation should someday be built back up to the point at which it could be a strong American ally, but he had little aptitude for being part of that arduous process. He was a soldier and he knew that was all that he was. He belonged where the fighting was.

Moreover, Patton did not like the way he saw events progressing in Europe. The destruction of Germany had upset the overall balance of power on the continent. Into the resulting vacuum was moving the Soviet Union. Patton had been suspicions of Soviet intentions for a long time, and the recent weeks had only intensified his suspicions. It was with the Russians in mind that he urged Eisenhower to go all the way to Berlin. It was with the Russians in mind that he wanted the American army to meet the Soviet army as far to the east as possible. He believed that whatever territory the Russian army took from the German army in central and Eastern Europe, they would have no intention of turning loose. Winston Churchill also harbored great suspicions about the intentions of the Soviet Union, but these two voices were lost in the chorus of allied solidarity and the determination of the Combined Chiefs of Staff to make military policy independent of political considerations. While the new American President, Harry Truman, would share a similar tendency to desire a more forceful stance with the Soviet Union, by the time he began to shape policy decisions, the situation on the ground in Europe had already solidified.

Patton accepted an invitation to meet with Russian officers and troops in the German town of Linz and took part in several ceremonies of triumph. There was much drinking, but Patton insisted on drinking whiskey instead of the vodka for which his hosts were famous. He obviously was very concerned about getting drunk and happily boasted that he made it through everything without even a headache. He was presented with a medal, "The Order of Kutuzov," which was a very prestigious honor in the Russian army. His soldier's eye took in every detail as his Russian hosts whisked him from place to place and palace to palace. He saw an army marked by "severe discipline," and officers that frankly struck him as "having the appearance of recently civilized Mongolian bandits." His aide, Hap Gay felt similarly. "Everything they did impressed one with the idea of virility and cruelty," Gay wrote. All that Patton saw confirmed his suspicions. "They give me the impression of something that is to be feared in future world political reorganization."

As for the future of the world's political organization, Patton was skeptical. All the political talk that was circulating about creating a new international organization called the United Nations to keep the peace struck Patton as foolish. He dismissed the idea as nuts. "As long as man is man," he said, "there will be war, and the only way to avoid trouble is to have the best Army and Navy, which we now have." No form of a "league for security" as he called it would be able to dissuade an aggressor from action. Only the strong threat of force could do that, and that applied to the Soviet Union in Europe as much as any nation. Since Patton felt that the United States now had the best army and navy, and outperformed the Russians in artillery, air power, and tanks, he believed that now was the time to act. "If it should be necessary to fight the Russians," which he believed was growing inevitable, "the sooner we do it the better." He thought that before it came to a fight, though, the Russians would back down.

First things first, however. Patton was going back to the United States. In June he flew to Boston, and was greeted there at the airport by Beatrice and their three children. It was a joyous reunion, of course, full of kissing, hugging, and tears of happy relief. He got to spend time with his grandchildren. His family was not the only people who were happy to see him. The road from the airport to downtown was packed with a crowd estimated at one million. It was the biggest such reception in the history of Boston. Downtown at the band shell along the Charles River, 20,000 people, including 400 wounded veterans of the Third Army, waited for him in eager anticipation. He said a few words to the cheering throng and saluted the men who had fought under his command. After a dinner that evening and his first night back in the states in years, Patton and Beatrice headed to Denver and then to Los Angeles, both of which had welcome rallies for him to attend. Everyone, it seemed, wanted to see General George Patton, scourge of the Nazis.

Back on the east coast, he met with army leaders at the Pentagon and the president at the White House. He learned that it was very unlikely he would be going to the Pacific to fight the Japanese and he was disappointed. All the emotion of these days, all the cheering crowds, had left him exhausted and drained. As was his custom, he went to the hospital to visit wounded soldiers. When he went to see some veterans at the Walter Reed Army Hospital's amputee ward, he burst into tears, telling them "if I had been a better general, most of you wouldn't be here." The stress and uncertainty over his future was weighing heavily on him.

In a month, he was back in Europe with his soldiers. He felt more comfortable among them than he had at home in the United States. His men gave him a grand welcoming ceremony. Tanks and soldiers lined the roads down which he rode. Despite the frustrations that occupation duty caused him and the nagging sense that no one understood the real complexion of the postwar American-Soviet competition but him, he was happy to be back. "It gave me a very warm feeling in my heart to be back among soldiers," he said. He would not be returning to America.

Chapter 12

IT IS FINISHED

If it be my lot to die, let me do so with courage and honor in a manner which will bring the greatest harm to the enemy, and please, oh Lord, protect and guide those I shall leave behind. Give us the victory, Lord.

George Patton spent the next few months in Europe growing more bitter and more convinced that the Allies were making a huge mistake by letting the Russians get their way on apparently every issue. The frustration that he felt from the current talk of demobilization, the notion of collective security and the allied willingness to trust the Russians continued to roil in his mind. He saw little hope for the future. Barbaric Russians would overrun Europe and the United States would do nothing to stop it. All of Europe would soon be communist, he feared, and then it may well spread to the United States. At every turn, Patton believed he saw evidence of a horrible future unfolding before him. Only he could see it, he felt. Nobody else shared his opinions. A trip to Berlin depressed him even more, though the city was not quite as devastated as he thought it would be.

In the region of Bavaria, Patton was personally in charge of a policy called denazification, in which every person who had been a member of the German Nazi Party—the Americans discovered that was about 75 percent of the nation's population—would be removed from positions of power, authority, or responsibility of any sort. If a person had been a member of the Nazi party, he or she could not even work as a telephone or telegraph operator. It was a tough task, since Patton was also charged with ensuring that basic civil services were restored as soon as possible. Never-theless, Eisenhower was absolutely adamant on the point "regardless of the fact that we may sometimes suffer from local administrative effi-ciency." Ike believed without hesitation that "victory is not complete until we have eliminated from positions of responsibility and, in appro-priate cases properly punished, every active adherent to the Nazi party." Every last vestige of the Nazi party was to be eradicated and Eisenhower expected that this policy would be followed to the letter no less than one of his military orders during the war. He expected Patton to make sure his own subordinates were carrying it out at once and with no hesitation. He told Patton that "the discussional stage of this question is long past and any expressed opposition to the faithful execution of this order cannot be regarded leniently by me." That applied to Patton, too.

Patton's visceral hatred of communists and their threat to Europe caused him to turn a blind eye to the record of Nazi totalitarianism. The purge of the Nazis was proceeding too quickly, he thought, leaving un-trained, incapable administrators in charge of the only nation that could be a bulwark of defense against Soviet expansionism. He wanted the process to go more slowly. "I had never heard that we fought to de-natzify Germany—live and learn. What we are doing is to utterly de-stroy the only semi-modern state in Europe so that Russia can swallow the whole." As he began to suspect that Jewish politicians and interna-tional figures like Henry Morganthau and Bernard Baruch had hatched a plan to exact limitless revenge on every German, his opinions took on a decidedly anti-Semitic tone. Patton's tendency to see post-war Europe as a choice between supporting the Germans or the Russians—either supporting ex-Nazis or current communists—caused him to be more and more opposed to the policy of cleaning out every last former Nazi and suspicious of many who insisted on the practice. The tactics involved seemed more like something the Gestapo at its peak of power would have done than something American soldiers should be doing. The press, too, seemed to have lost its concept of justice, if indeed it ever had one, and felt "that a man can be kicked out because somebody else says he is a Nazi." Patton told the press that it struck him that nobody should be removed from a job or have property confiscated "without the suc-cessful proof of guilt before a court of law." It seemed to him that throughout the last 15 years or so, it was "no more possible for a man to be a civil servant in Germany and not have paid lip service to Nazism than it is for a man to be a postmaster in American and not have paid lip service to the Democratic Party or Republican Party when it is in power."

He said much the same thing to a combative group of reporters in September. Almost immediately it began appearing in the newspapers that Patton disapproved of the denazification policy and that Patton had compared Nazis to Republicans and Democrats. The whole affair deteriorated into an unpleasant contest of who said what, exactly. From every direction there was a slightly different story. Reporters followed him around constantly. In a press conference late in September, Patton tried to explain what he had meant in every instance in which he had commented on the policies of the occupying army, but it seemed to do no good. The question-and-answer sessions with reporters always got away from him. He never said the right thing. There probably was no right thing he could have said.

Patton was constantly dejected. "The more I see of people," he wrote in his diary one night, "I regret that I survived the war." Later he said that the "great tragedy of my life was that I survived the last battle." When Eisenhower began hearing these growing rumbles again sowed by George Patton's latest statements, he summoned Patton to his headquarters. "This man is yet going to drive me to drink," Ike told his wife. "He misses more good opportunities to keep his mouth shut than almost anyone I ever knew."

All of Patton's successes and his world-wide fame as an effective general were not enough to prepare him for his post-war role as a military governor, trying to carry out policies that to him made little sense and seemed utterly blind to a greater danger that was rising up in the ruins of the war. All through his career he had gotten into trouble because he so singularly focused on the immediate task at hand and disregarded everything he deemed extraneous. His emotions, informed and intimately shaped by a lifetime of the study of war, were his guide as a leader and they had rarely failed him in the heat of the action. He had no knack for politics, though, and never pretended to have. But now, at the end of his career, he was forced to think through every possible sentence and its ramifications before he spoke. He had to be political. He was accustomed to barking orders and having them obeyed. If they were not obeyed, someone would immediately feel his wrath. He was accustomed to action. Now the lack of it made him uneasy, unhappy, and uncertain of his future. He had the growing horrible sense that he had literally out-lived his usefulness. "Last time a war ended I wrote a poem," he told Beatrice, "Now I feel too low." "Another war has ended and with it my usefulness to the world."

At the end of September, Eisenhower removed Patton from command of the Third Army. His old subordinate Lucien Truscott was to take his place. Now Patton was the head of the Fifteenth Army, which consisted just of a small headquarters unit charged with writing up a history of the army's operations in Europe. On a rainy day in October, the transfer of command ceremony took place in a gymnasium.

George Patton's last headquarters was in the German town of Bad Nauheim. From there he watched the army occupation of Germany in a detached way and watched his staff push papers around the office. He saw Eisenhower regularly and was annoyed by him much of the time. As they were photographed together at a football game, Patton was struck by the overwhelming sense that Eisenhower wanted to be the president of the United States, and his opinion of his old friend completely deteriorated. When fan mail began arriving from the United States, it cheered him up to a certain degree. He planned to finish out the year in his current position and then retire, after which he intended to speak his mind without reservation and constantly, because "America needs some honest men who dare to say what they think, not what they think people want them to think." "I know I am right," he said, "and the rest can go to Hell or I hope they can but it is going to be very crowded." By December, he had made plans to head back to the United States for good. He booked a transatlantic passage on the U.S.S. *New York* for the second week of the month.

One of the few activities that gave Patton pleasure was hunting. When he was stationed in Bavaria, he had gone hunting on the Czechoslovakian ancestral estate of a Prince who was one of the only generals "who ever defeated Napoleon on the field of battle before Waterloo," he carefully noted in his diary. Around Bad Nauheim there was good pheasant hunting and Hap Gay suggested that they take advantage of it before Patton headed back to the states. Patton thought it a splendid idea and decided to spend his last day in Germany hunting. It would be a great way to end his European duty with a memory other than with disagreeable paperwork or simply sitting at his headquarters, mad at the world. On Sunday, December 9, Patton and Gay, along with a driver, a private named Horace Woodring, loaded up a big 1938 Cadillac limousine and headed out. There were even some ruins of a Roman outpost on the way to where they were going, and they took a quick detour to see them.

Just before noon, in a suburb north of Mannheim, a big truck that was headed toward Patton's car on the opposite side of the road suddenly turned in front of them. "Sit tight!" yelled Gay, who was sitting in the front seat next to the driver. The driver wrenched the steering wheel to the left, but the car slammed into the right side of the truck. Patton's car was going about 30 miles an hour, the truck about 10. The right front fender and the radiator of the car were smashed. The truck was not seriously damaged. Both Gay and Woodring were unhurt.

Patton, however, had been sitting on the edge of the roomy back seat at the moment of the accident and the force of the impact threw him violently forward. He struck his head on the partition between the front and rear seats. The impact nearly scalped him, tearing the skin back from his forehead, but far more seriously, it damaged his spinal cord, fracturing and dislocating two vertebrae. Gay immediately got in the back seat to check on Patton who was bleeding but conscious. "I think I'm paralyzed," Patton whispered. It took an hour for an ambulance to arrive and get him to the nearest hospital, which had once been, ironically enough, a German cavalry school. He could not move anything below his shoulders.

By the time Patton got to the hospital, he was slipping into shock and his blood pressure was falling. Doctors put stitches in his head to close the laceration, but could do little to repair his spinal injury. Several neurosurgeons were called in to examine Patton including one from the United States. They immobilized his spine and attached a gruesome mechanism of hooks to his face to stretch his spine and alleviate the pressure between the vertebrae. The pain from these hooks secured under his cheekbones must have been nearly unbearable, and he had almost no other sensation as he lay helplessly in his hospital bed. When Beatrice arrived in the afternoon on December 11, Patton's spirits picked up a little. Gradually, however, the doctors came to the unavoidable conclusion that Patton would never walk again, or even move under his own power. He demanded to know their prognosis without any sugarcoating. "What chance have I to ride a horse again?" the old cavalryman asked. "None," said the doctor flatly. He thanked the doctor for his honesty.

"I'll try to be a good patient," Patton told the doctors, and as much as was possible, he kept up a good attitude. The hospital was inundated with cards and flowers and concerned well-wishers from the moment word got out of what had happened. Well-wishers included Eisenhower, Truman, Marshall, Bradley, and innumerable common folk, many of whom had either served under Patton at one time, had children who served under him, or even knew him only through the stories of his exploits. Beatrice kept up a cheerful attitude as much as she possibly could. The fatigue was grueling. Gradually, though, more problems began to appear. He was having trouble breathing because his lungs were becoming obstructed. He had to now wear an oxygen mask some of the time. His heart began to have trouble as fluid gathered in his chest. Even though from time to time his vital signs seemed to improve, his overall condition sank steadily.

Some time in the early evening of December 21, George Patton died in his sleep. The doctors listed the cause of death as "pulmonary edema and congestive heart failure." They moved his body downstairs to a basement that was once the site of horse stalls while they waited for a coffin to arrive. Beatrice would not let them perform an autopsy and insisted that Patton be buried here in Europe, rather than be taken back to the United States. She knew that "George would want to lie beside the men of his army who have fallen." Patton himself had earlier insisted that should he die overseas, "In God's name don't bring my body home." He had said that it "would be far more pleasant to my ghostly future to lie among my soldiers than to rest in the sanctimonious precincts of a civilian cemetery."

Newspapers all around the world announced his death in somber headlines. There was an overwhelming sense of grief all over Europe, wherever there were American or British soldiers. Soldiers of every rank wrote little memorials to Patton in their letters home, or in touching notes of sympathy to Beatrice. A detachment from the Fifteenth Cavalry Regiment escorted his coffin to a church in Heidelburg for a service. A chaplain read Patton's two favorite Psalms: the Sixty-third and the Ninetieth. A train carried his coffin westward to the American military cemetery in Hamm, Luxembourg, a small suburb of the city that had been Patton's headquarters during the Battle of the Bulge. His grave was next to a Third Army soldier who had been killed in that battle. In a constant rain, his coffin was lowered into the ground.

AFTERWORD

Had George Patton lived for very long after the end of World War II, he would have been infuriated to see the very circumstances he warned of in his last days coming true with alarming rapidity. The onset of the Cold War between the United States and the Soviet Union against the backdrop of a divided Europe was precisely the situation he dreaded. Perhaps he could have taken a little comfort in the fact that in the face of this, American troops did not completely pull out of western Germany and remained in place as a bulwark against further Soviet expansionism. (One has to be curious, too, about what Patton's reaction would have been to another correct prediction on his part—the presidency of his old friend Dwight Eisenhower.)

He correctly foresaw that the days of an isolationist United States had to come to an end after the war. With the march of technology, the Atlantic and Pacific Oceans no longer provided safe insulation from threats. "They now say that we've got 3,000 miles of ocean," to protect America, he said in 1945, "but 20 years from now this 3,000 miles of ocean will be just a good spit. This is a very serious thing, and many people don't visualize this very grave danger," he warned. He knew what Hitler's V-2 rockets had been able to achieve during the war, raining explosives down on London. Even though they were not militarily effective, they were a weapon that struck terror in the hearts of the British. Part of their terror came from the way they would hit without any warning at all. No air raid sirens could anticipate a supersonic missile and they were part of the future of combat. Patton also saw that they were effective enough to influence military policy. In the drive up to the German border, supplies had been taken from him and given to Montgomery's forces because Churchill insisted that those missile bases be put out of action immediately.

In addition to his fear of the traditional American desire to demobilize rapidity after the end of a war, Patton worried that the new atomic bomb would make this even more precipitous. The use of the two atomic bombs to bring the war with Japan to a quicker end was a mistake, he thought; not for what it did to Japan, but for how it made ill-informed Americans think. He knew that people would use the bomb "to state that the Army, Navy, and Air Forces are no longer necessary as this bomb will either prevent war or destroy the human race." It was just another weapon, he said—"a new instrument added to the orchestra of death which is war." War, regardless of the advent of new weaponry, would always be with us. He had seen the horse replaced by the tank. He had seen airplanes and missiles fill the skies over the battlefield. Nothing had really changed, though. There was nothing new under the sun.

Patton was a man who seemed to be wrapped up in contradictions. He was a foul-mouthed man who exhorted his armies to kill mercilessly and relentlessly, but who also was a deeply religious man who read the Bible and who would storm out of a room if someone told a vulgar joke he thought inappropriate or he was exposed to behavior he judged immoral. He spent his life training for war and loved to be in the thick of the battle more than anywhere else, but tried his hardest to bring war to the quickest end possible. He knew that being a good leader meant also being a good actor. He slapped his soldiers and cried over their wounds. He recognized that war was a horrific spectacle but nowhere on earth was there more valor, bravery, and selfless sacrifice than in the horror of battle. He also knew how hard it was for American boys to become soldiers and exactly what it took to lead them into battle.

In the years after his death, George Patton became an American legend and a figure that continues to captivate. He serves to remind us of one of the darker facts of life with which we must contend. He reminds us that wars will come, and it is the responsibility of the military commander to see that when it does, it gets finished as quickly as possible. And the way in which Patton fits into military history reminds all of us of just how different the job of a military leader in combat is from what most of us do in our peaceful day-to-day lives.

BIBLIOGRAPHIC ESSAY

To say that there are many books about General George S. Patton, Jr. is a tremendous understatement. From biography to books on business tactics to studies of leadership and military theory, no matter how a reader would like to approach Patton, there is a book to guide the way. Many seem to idolize him and almost as many seem to want to tear him down. Such is probably inevitable with a public persona as he had. All serious study of Patton, though, should begin with Carlo D'Este's exhaustive *Patton: A Genius for War*, a hefty volume that paints as full a picture of Patton as we are likely to ever have. Its tone is sympathetic, but it makes no attempt to downplay or cover over any of Patton's shortcomings. It is also one of the best sources for the early history of the Patton family. Also, its postscript on Patton, his image and legacy, is an especially penetrating essay that wraps up the man nicely. The reader of D'Este's book must not miss reading it. Also simply indispensable for the serious student of Patton are Martin Blumenson's two volumes of *The Patton Papers*. Blumenson, who served at Third Army's headquarters in early 1945, has taken the voluminous writings of Patton and used them to tell the General's life story in his own words. Each volume is nearly a thousand pages long and provides a comprehensive look at Patton that is unequalled anywhere else. Blumenson has also written a good short biography gleaned from his study of Patton entitled *Patton: The Man Behind the Legend, 1885–1945*. George Patton's own *War As I Knew It* is a distillation of his writings from his time in action in World War II. *Before the Colors Fade: Portrait of a Soldier* is an older volume written by Patton's nephew Frederick Ayer, Jr. Patton's aide Charles Codman wrote a book about his experiences with Patton entitled

Drive, but both this and the Ayer book are very tough to find today. Roger Nye's informative *The Patton Mind: The Professional Development of an Extraordinary Leader*, looks at the way Patton's love of books and his study of military theory and history shaped him. Herbert Essame's *Patton as a Military Commander* focuses primarily on Patton's generalship. A more recent entry is *General Patton: A Soldier's Life*, by Stanley P. Hirshson, that seems to work hard to set itself apart from the other works with limited success. A more unique volume is George Forty's *The Armies of George S. Patton*. Forty's book is more of a user's guide to the Third Army, and provides a useful supplement to a biography like that of D'Este. It explains the organizational make-up of the Third Army, Patton's staffs, the weapons of the time, and provides short biographical entries on most of the primary officers and aides who served under Patton's command. There are any number of books that purport to adapt Patton's military beliefs to the business world. *Patton on Leadership*, *Patton's One-Minute Messages*, and *General Patton's Principles: For Life and Leadership*, are just three of them.

Victor Davis Hanson writes about Patton in a particularly enlightening way in *The Soul of Battle: From Ancient Times to the Present Day, How Three Great Liberators Vanquished Tyranny*. One-third of the book looks at Patton's leadership of the Third Army and its crusade to liberate Germany from the Nazis. It talks about the particular crusading element present in Patton's actions and how this ideology informed him and his army, making them so effective. One also comes across many useful accounts and anecdotes of Patton in Dwight Eisenhower's World War II memoir, *Crusade in Europe*, as well as in Omar Bradley's *A Soldier's Story*. Grandson Robert Patton has written *The Pattons: A Person History of an American Family* that takes a broader look at the whole Patton family tree.

On the Internet there is much information about George Patton; some sites are worthwhile, some are not. The Patton Museum of Cavalry and Armor at Fort Knox maintains a good little site at http://knox-www.army. mil/museum/gspatton.htm. It has an especially good bibliography. The site of Patton's Desert Training Center in California has a museum and a website at http://www.desertusa.com/mag99/feb/stories/ paton.html. The Virginia Military Institute has a good webpage on the Patton family that talks about all the Patton's who attended VMI at http://www.vmi.edu /archives/patton.html. All of the on-line encyclopedias have entries about Patton. Typing "George S. Patton" into a search engine returns literally thousands of sites.

INDEX

About the Author

DAVID A. SMITH is a Lecturer in History at Baylor University.